"It Was Play or Starve"

"It Was Play or Starve": Acting in the Nineteenth-Century American Popular Theatre

John Hanners

Bowling Green State University Popular Press

Bowling Green, Ohio 43403

Entertainment and Leisure Studies

Series Editors

Michael T. Marsden

Ray B. Browne

Contents

Acknowledgments

"It Was Play or Starve" in slightly different form was published in *Theatre Research International* 8 (1982). Reprinted with permission.

"William Henry Lane, 'Master Juba' " in different form was published in *Consumable Goods II: Papers from the North East Popular Culture Association Meeting*. Reprinted with permission.

Portions of material published in *Traces* 2:2 (Spring 1990) with the title of "The Great Wizard of the North" are reprinted with permission.

"The Professional Stock Company in Terre Haute, Indiana" appeared in different form in *Theatre History* Studies 12 (June 1992). Reprinted with permission.

Portions of material published in *Theatre Survey* 23:2 (Nov. 1982) with the title of "Vicissitude and Woe: The Theatrical Misadventures of John Banvard" are reprinted with permission.

Portions of material published in *Indiana History Bulletin* 59:4 (April 1982) with the title of "Edwin Booth in Terre Haute, Indiana" is reprinted with permission.

"The Great Three-Mile Printing: John Banvard's Mississippi Panorama" was printed in the *Journal of American Culture* 4:1 (Spring 1981). Reprinted with permission.

Preface

In 1845, Mrs. Anna Cora Mowatt, 26 years old, wealthy New York socialite and author of America's first significant native stage comedy, *Fashion*, found herself, due to her ailing husband's financial reversals, in reduced circumstances. This respectable woman, in an act unprecedented for someone of her social standing, took to the New York stage as an actress, earning both a living and wide acclaim. Then, cashing in on her success, she launched a profitable tour of the American provincial theatre and in doing so, encountered an alien culture unlike any she had known in New York. For one thing, she complained, no one told her how hard the life would be. Provincial stock company actors often rehearsed from eight in the morning until that evening's curtain; a constant change of bill was necessary to satisfy hungry and easily jaded audiences and actors often opened a play after a single rehearsal. In the midst of this chaotic atmosphere, Mrs. Mowatt, sickly most of her life, managed to memorize 15 major roles, one of which, the title character in Nicholas Rowe's three-hour drama *The Tragedy of Jane Shore*, she learned in less than 24 hours. She fell desperately ill, dozed off onstage, and put up with drunken actors working alongside her. The misery was unrelenting. She mistakenly swallowed a bottle of ink instead of her prop poison, struggled with shoddy, ill-fitting costumes, and wildly improvised when other actors forgot their lines, an all too common occurrence in the provincial theatre. The dizzying pace nearly killed her before Mrs. Mowatt learned what dozens of lesser lights before her already knew— the life of the nineteenth-century popular entertainer outside the relatively safe enclaves of New York, Boston and Philadelphia was a hardscrabble existence, fraught with uncertainty and peril. But then a wondrous thing occurred. Fortified by her Swedenborgian beliefs, a sweet nature and an unrelenting passion for doing theatre, she found herself growing stronger, not weaker, in body and spirit. The excitement and danger of performance, the thunderous applause, the long rehearsals, the hazardous travel—all the formidable challenges of frontier theatre— invigorated her. It wasn't long, she later wrote, before "my health,

1

instead of failing entirely, as was predicted, visibly improved."

The deleterious effects of late hours were counteracted by constant exercise, an animating, exhilarating pursuit, and the all-important *nepenth* of inner peace. I gained new vigor and elasticity. With additional burden came the added strength whereby it could be bourne. (qtd. Barnes 160)

In the midst of theatrical adversity, Anna Cora Mowatt was born anew.

This book relates experiences of selected individuals and groups who, like Anna Cora Mowatt, were associated with popular theatre in nineteenth-century America and who demonstrated remarkable resiliency while suffering personal and professional vicissitudes in struggling to bring a variety of amusements to the urban setting and to out-of-the-way places. The focus here is relatively narrow and concentrates on narrative biography rather than the presentation of a comprehensive overview of the social history of the period's mass entertainments. For the latter the reader must look elsewhere, and numerous references throughout the text will serve as excellent guides to such study.

Because these subjects belong to an age in which the line between popular entertainment and "what later became to be called 'legitimate' theatre was not always clear" (McNamara 14), the reader will find Edwin Booth, the great touring tragedian, and Adele Sandrock, the fine German classical actress, in the same pages as "John Johannes, The Great Wizard of the North" and Mr. King, the "Great American Fire-Eater." Most wandered the Western rivers, those great stretches of water that included the Ohio, Missouri and Mississippi, as well as tributaries like the Cumberland, Tennessee, Wabash, and Allegheny. They moved westward as the century wore on "in step with the population across the continent" (Grimsted 87). They traveled on the waterways, by railroad and, even more treacherously, overland. Only the showman, lamented harried circus manager W.C. Coup, could understand "the volume of dread hardship and disaster held by those two small words, 'bad roads' " (76).

"Bad roads," social as well as natural ones, will be a recurring theme. Professional entertainers throughout the nineteenth century were social pariahs. Their exotic dress and lifestyle and their reputation, usually undeserved, for licentious and scandalous behavior, put them beyond the pale of normal society. This, the historical lot of all theatre folk, should come as no surprise in a nineteenth century imbued with religious evangelical fervor and rigid moral and racial codes. The road to social respectability was not an easy one. The stage was looked upon as a place of evil, a breeding ground for sin that all decent people avoided. Typical were family reactions to frontier actor-manager Noah Ludlow's decision to enter show business: "My mother's grief was very great, my sister drooped and became melancholy, my brother Joseph said but little, and seemed unwilling to talk to me...my brother John...said...that he was done with me forever!" (Ludlow 7).

Paradoxically, the more entertainers were rejected by society, the more they sought middle-class acceptance, the more they hungered for recognition as serious artists engaged in a serious business. Edwin Booth founded The Player's Club, in front of which his formidable statue stands to this day, to "exalt the standard of personal worth among the actors of America" (Kimmel 323). H.L. Bateman put on the gentlemanly airs of an aristocrat across two continents, belying his rough show business origins on the frontier by associating with the cream of London society. John Banvard ingratiated himself among the New York and Boston social and political elite in the vain hope that he would be accepted as an equal, a wealthy patron of the arts rather than a hack playwright and a mediocre painter. The saddest case is perhaps the African-American singer and dancer William Henry Lane, doubly cast out, rejected first by a racist society at large and then shunned by the white minstrel fraternity to which he sought admittance.

One other thing unites the professional entertainers in this book beyond peripatetic lives and social ostracization. Like Mrs. Mowatt, they were in it for the money. They labored hard to perfect their craft and spent long days, weeks and months to "work up" their acts, but the bottom line was that they did it for a living. The most unabashed pursuers of money were, of course, the circus grifters, whose sole purpose in life was to separate suckers from their cash. But others were just as motivated by profit, regardless of their stated intentions in various memoirs, reminiscences and authorized biographies. John Banvard's showboats, mammoth panorama painting and theatre-museum were conceived and executed to make their creator rich. H.L. and Sidney Bateman thrust their infant daughters on stage in adult Shakespearean roles because they knew a moneymaking novelty act when they saw one. Edwin Booth wound up playing Hamlet in the provinces while engaged in a fierce but ultimately futile battle to stave off personal bankruptcy. William Henry Lane literally sang for his supper in the slum-ridden Five Points Section of New York; poverty, a poor diet and overwork eventually killed him. The Terre Haute, Indiana, stock companies and the European psuedo "Meininger" troupe did everything in their power to wrest a living from progressively disastrous circumstances.

Thus, we must not romanticize nor sentimentalize these individuals too much. They were quite capable, in a century known for its sentimentality, of doing that for themselves. The fact is, they were often unpleasant people—physical violence, gunplay and even murder were not unknown—and their "art" was often amateurish, slipshod and haphazard by modern standards. Neither should we judge them too harshly. They simply did the best they could with the cards they were dealt. Despite the condescension of theatrical and literary critics who judge an era by the permanence of its written drama, they are worthy of our respect and fit subjects for closer examination because itinerant popular entertainers represent the one continuum in Western theatre history. From the Atellan *farceurs* of third-century Naples to the "new" vaudevillians of the late twentieth century, versatile actors—the acrobats, the magicians, the jugglers, the singing comedians—are always waiting in the wings, ready to present fresh material to new audiences in unfamiliar places. The following pages tell stories about nineteenth-century American entertainers, but their behavior, attitudes, and outlook on life probably differ little from the members of Shakespeare's company, the wandering sixteenth-century *commedia dell'arte* players, or even Arion (c. 625-585 B.C.) himself, the ancient Greek strolling entertainer, a harpist by trade, who, if popular tradition is to be believed, labeled his fellow players *tragoidi* and his improvised songs and dances *tragikon drama*, thereby inventing tragedy.

Sources for this study came from a variety of places and primary works and artifacts are used wherever possible. Contemporary newspapers, both in the larger theatre centers (New York, Boston, St. Louis, Milwaukee) and in small towns (particularly Terre Haute, Indiana) provided a regional perspective on audience reactions, as well as valuable narrative detail. Unpublished diaries and autobiographies, account books, scrapbooks, manuscripts, and legal documents were also used. Much of Chapter 9 is based on personal interviews. The study is indebted, as all such work must be, to dozens of other scholars whose efforts have resulted in what is now a considerable body of work on nineteenth-century popular culture. The reader will find acknowledgment of their work in the references.

Numerous individuals and agencies aided in the research and writing of this book. The National Endowment for the Humanities, the Allegheny College Faculty Development Fund and the East Texas State University Office of Graduate Studies and Research provided funds for various stages of this work. Several libraries, research centers and individuals shared valuable primary source materials, including Professor Donald R. Cressey; the Division of Archives and Manuscripts, Minnesota Historical Society; Emeline Fairbanks Memorial Library, Terre Haute, Indiana; Hatcher Graduate Library, University of Michigan; the New Workingmen's Library, New Harmony, Indiana; Historical Resource Center, South Dakota Department of Education and Cultural Affairs; Watertown Regional Library, Watertown, South Dakota; and the Vigo County Historical Society, Terre Haute, Indiana.

My colleagues Nels G. Juleus, Anthony J. Buckley, Bruce L. Clayton, and James C. Bulman all provided encouragement and criticism. Julia Curtis, Georg Schuttler and the late Gerald Sullivan generously shared their knowledge of and interest in nineteenth-century American theatre with me. Samantha Stephens read, proofed and generally displayed a gentle patience with the early stages of this manuscript.

Portions of Chapter 1, 4, 5, 6, and 7 have appeared in *Theatre Research International, Indiana History Bulletin, Traces: A Magazine of Indiana and Midwestern History, Theatre History Studies, Theatre Survey,* and *Journal of American Culture* and are published here by permission in revised form.

A special thanks goes to the circus workers, most of whom are now deceased, who shared their memories of the circus and circus grift with Nels G. Juleus and me.

And finally, Lou, Lisa and Michael Hanners initially suggested this work and then patiently read, listened and prodded until it was completed.

Part One

Showboats, Minstrels and Panoramas

Chapter 1
"It Was Play or Starve":
An Early Showboat Entertainer

Theatre chronicles from the early nineteenth-century American frontier provide the modern reader with rich and varied insights into the lives of itinerant entertainers who practiced their trade while battling bad weather, poor traveling conditions, fickle audiences, and a hostile clergy and press. Some of these accounts have become minor classics in Americana. Solomon Smith's *Theatrical Apprenticeship* (1845), Noah Ludlow's *Dramatic Life As I Found It* (1880), and Joseph Jefferson's *Autobiography* (1890), for instance, all offer fascinating, if often unsubstantiated, anecdotes about theatre in the backwoods and backwaters of the Ohio and Mississippi River Valleys before their authors eventually achieved fame and fortune in larger theatre centers such as Cincinnati, Louisville, St. Louis, New Orleans, and the, then as now, nation's theatrical capital, New York City.

But no performers were more resolute—or in retrospect, more foolhardy—than the band of intrepid actors led by John Banvard (1815-1891) down the Wabash River in 1834 and again in 1835. Banvard's experience is worth a closer look. Personal accounts such as Ludlow, Smith and Jefferson's have come down to us because those managers and actors were eventually *successful* and enjoyed lengthy careers. Banvard's early life, on the other hand, with its unequal share of disasters and triumphs and its hard labor for little reward, serves as a paradigm for those hundreds of wandering anonymous entertainers, all pioneers in their own way, who lived and died on the Western rivers without ever having their story told.

John Banvard was born on November 15, 1815 in New York City.[1] He was the 11th and last child of Daniel Banvard, co-owner with William Hollinsead of a prosperous construction company that numbered among its regular clients the Lorrillard Brothers, the famous tobacconists. His mother, Elizabeth Mead, was the Connecticut daughter of an original "minute man."[2] The Banvard home was a spacious, two-story structure at the corner of Broadway and Canal Street (Heilbron 108), and it was there that young John, through the enthusiastic encouragement of his parents, developed an intense interest in art, poetry and science. He learned the basics of chemistry from his schoolmaster John Griscom (1774-1852), prominent Quaker and America's first teacher of chemistry. John's first experiment, trying to collect hydrogen in a glass tube, blew up in his face. For years afterward he suffered from poor eyesight and from the effects of bright sunlight.[3]

In 1831, his father Daniel suffered a paralyzing stroke. William Hollinsead, Daniel's business partner, fellow church deacon and best friend, liquidated in Daniel's absence all the construction firm's assets, fled New York, and was never seen again. Daniel, stunned by this turn of events, suffered a second stroke and died. The family was left destitute. The death of his father and the subsequent family humiliation—the house and all its furnishings were sold at a sheriff's auction—followed Banvard all the rest of his life. Daniel's funeral bill, which the family was unable to pay, read "one coffin $12, one shroud $1, 5 yds. cloth $2.19, 3/4 yd. black muslin .33, total $15.51." This tiny scrap of paper, with its poignant one-cent error, was among John Banvard's few personal possessions when he himself died in 1891.[4]

In the fall of 1832, at age 16, Banvard struck out for Louisville, where his older brother Daniel Jr. and his wife Jane had settled. Banvard had no trade and no prospects, but he was a strapping youth, unusually tall for his age, with striking grey eyes, dark brown hair and fair skin. Louisville was a sprawling, thriving frontier town with an important riverfront on the Ohio. A special census that year disclosed a population of 10,366, a 260 percent increase over a decade before (Kendrick). It was a city full of promise for a young man making his way in the world and Banvard soon found work at an apothecary's store. He didn't keep the job for long, though. In the spring of 1833 he was fired for drawing unflattering caricatures of his employer on the store walls. Chagrined by his firing, but now confident in his artistic skills, Banvard became an itinerant artist, an occupation that he pursued on and off for the next 14 years.

The itinerant artist was a fixture on the American frontier and most, like Banvard, were self-taught. They usually worked in more than one mode, including miniatures, clay modeling, *fractur* (illuminated

Fig. 1. John Banvard, 1834. A sketch by John P. Frankenstein, German immigrant and, like Banvard, an itinerant Western artist. *Minnesota Historical Society.* Reprinted with permission.

handwriting), sign painting, silhouettes, frescoes, and the interior decoration of public halls. Even the best American artists from 1750 to 1840, men like Benjamin West, John Singleton Copley, Gilbert Stuart (portrait painter of George Washington), Charles Willson Peale, and John James Audubon, moved restlessly from town to town in search of work, any kind of work (Wright 129, 132). No Banvard paintings from this period survive, so his talent is impossible to judge. He did, however, open a portrait studio that quickly failed, as did his efforts at finding work as a scene painter in the Louisville theatres.

Desperate for work, Banvard went down to the Louisville docks and unloaded barges. There he chanced to meet William Chapman, Sr. (1764-1839) and his family, who hired him as scene painter for their showboat, America's very first, called *Chapman's Ark*, or more commonly, *The Floating Theatre*. Chapman and his sons, daughters and their families had immigrated from England in 1827 and they followed the Western rivers overland presenting Shakespeare, tragedies, farces, and musical entertainments. But license fees and hall rentals, when halls were available, drained the family's financial resources. Then Chapman struck upon the idea of avoiding fees altogether by performing *on* the rivers, thereby adapting an "eastern institution (the theatre) to the Western environment (dependence on the rivers)." The family outfitted a 100-foot long by 16-foot wide flatboat in Pittsburgh and quickly developed a seasonal routine. Launching their boat from a Pittsburgh landing, they drifted down the Ohio and Mississippi rivers and various tributaries to New Orleans, often starting their day at three o'clock in the morning to avoid heavy headwinds. They stopped at dozens of remote landings for one night stands during their arduous 1,800-mile journey. When they reached New Orleans, they dismantled the boat, sold the lumber, and with their accumulated capital, made their way overland to Pittsburgh where they would buy a new boat. When the business was more profitable in later years, they traveled from New Orleans to New York by steamer (Graham 13; Ford 123).

Early descriptions of *Chapman's Ark* make it out to be a sort of floating palace, but according to Banvard their 1833 craft was a crude affair, unlike the magnificent and ornamented vessels that plied the rivers later in the century and provide us with our modern image of the showboat. It was, said Banvard, "very rudely built. The staves that supported the roof were pinned onto the upright joists with large oak pins, and when a steamer would pass the heavy swells would cause the pins to creak in a horrid and discordant manner, sometimes very annoying to the audience."

The Chapmans, noted for their superb acting, emphasized regular drama more than any subsequent enterprise and set "the pattern for the American showboat...wherever they played, danced, and sang, they spread...charm and geniality" (Graham 21). However genial the atmosphere on board during performance, Banvard soon discovered that the Chapmans were less than genial to their hired help. This strange family, extremely tight-knit and clannish, suspicious of any outsider, was rumored to speak a secret language to one another in the presence of fellow theatre workers as well as strangers.

Halfway to New Orleans, William Chapman informed Banvard he didn't have enough money to pay him, but the young artist decided to stay on board until "such time as the management would accumulate enough funds so as to liquidate [my] claim." He took a space at the back of the stage left proscenium and boarded off an area in which to stand and sit. He then constructed a berth which extended underneath the stage left box seats that hung directly over the water. As the summer passed and he still hadn't been paid, Banvard discovered that his rigged cabin was dangerous. Cracked, warped, and unseasoned, the wooden boards at the back of the box seats had wide gaps that allowed heavy swells from passing steamers to douse Banvard day and night. During the winter he was constantly showered with icy water. One morning he woke up to discover that an early frost had completely frozen his bedding. When he sat up his blankets and bedspread broke in two and "stood straight up like a trap door." Determined to improve his lot, he stole some tar intended for the amphitheater roof, waited until the Chapmans were eating their supper, and then worked like "mad to patch" his "bedroom" wall.

Despite his uncomfortable accommodations, Banvard was smitten with the power, beauty, and as yet unspoiled wilderness of the Ohio and Mississippi rivers. He resolutely sketched river scenes and took careful notes concerning currents, bends, remote settlements and their inhabitants, and all the hazards and pitfalls that accompanied river travel. The experience with the Chapmans also inspired him to try his own hand at showboat theatre. The following season Banvard left the Chapmans and formed his own theatrical company, assembling it in July of 1834 at New Harmony on the Wabash River, that wide, shallow and muddy waterway that forms the boundary between Indiana and Illinois.

New Harmony, located on the Indiana side of the river, was the site of two major nineteenth-century social experiments. The first was established in the spring of 1815 by 56-year-old George Rapp on 25,000 acres where Rapp and his followers established a disciplined, celibate and thriving community under the auspices of a religious and economic dictatorship. The first buildings erected were separate dormitories for men and women. In 1825, Rapp sold the land to the British industrialist and great social reformer Robert Owen (1771-1858). Owen wanted to form a working socialist community to refute his critics' claims that such enterprises were impossible because of the nature of human greed. Twice Owen addressed the U.S. Congress in the presence of President John Quincy Adams and the Supreme Court Justices, pleading for land grants and spelling out in glowing terms his plans for a "Utopia on the Wabash." He planned to bring scientists, artists, and skilled laborers together in a perfect communal society. But in the end it just didn't work. "When production failed," according to historian R. Carlyle Buley, "meetings were held, resolutions passed. Much planning resulted, little work; it was a system under which the dissatisfied farmer might become a printer, bookkeeper, or teacher, the dissatisfied writer a farmer" (603, 605).

By late 1827, much of New Harmony had returned to private ownership. Despite its failure, however, New Harmony's list of "firsts" is impressive. In its short lifetime, the experiment produced America's first free public school system; first public trade school; first speed press (a machine that printed newspaper on a continuous sheet); first kindergarten; and its first woman's club (Wilson 62-81).

Now a budding 19-year-old entrepreneur, Banvard gathered together in this cultural oasis a motley collection of itinerant frontier performers, far less organized and less experienced at regular theatrical productions than the tightly-knit and disciplined Chapman clan. The group included Mr. Scudder, a "living statue" who was the "personification of motionless marble" and who dressed in "silk fleshings that fit to the skin and showed to advantage his faultless form;" Mr. King, "The Great American Fire-Eater," whose specialty was eating live coals and licking red hot iron;[5] and Mr. Mortimer, a comic actor, dancer, and tenor. Somehow Banvard also persuaded Mr. Wilbur, violinist, and Mr. Woodward, clarinetist, who made up the entire Chapman Family orchestra, to join him. A leather peddler by the name of Lowe signed on as the seventh and final member of the troupe after Banvard and Scudder conned him out of his life savings, an amount rumored in New Harmony to be $3,000 (Cox). Years later Banvard would claim Lowe was "induced" to join the troupe from the "great prospective profits held up to his view." The troupe then drew up an article of agreement, which every member dutifully signed, swearing to descend the rivers and "each in his separate and commonwealth capacity to do the best he could in his speciality and all money earned whatsoever was to go in a general fund and be divided once a week."

Banvard purchased a 40-foot, open apothecary's flatboat for one dollar per foot, a wise choice since apothecary boats had tightly sealed hulls to guard against water damage to its precious medicines. The company worked feverishly to complete their labors before winter ice made passage down the Wabash impossible. They built a large open-air auditorium that reportedly could seat as many as 200 spectators, and with the aid of Lowe's unanticipated capital, the actors purchased groceries, tobacco and cigars to sell along the river in case their theatrical ventures didn't pan out. Combining groceries and entertainment was also a clever idea. The floating grocery boat, flying a bright red flag, yellow if it also carried dry goods, was a common sight on the navigable frontier rivers. By mid-century as many as six a day passed even the remotest shoreline settlements (Wright 247).

Banvard rigged a seven-foot mechanized stage curtain that rose and fell and produced several scenic drops, spreading out his canvases in the large dining hall of the New Harmony Hotel, where the troupe stayed and where their board and lodging were a "very reasonable $1.50 a week." Banvard also billed himself as "John Johannas, The Great Wizard of the North," a title he undoubtedly borrowed from the well-known contemporary Scottish magician John Henry Anderson, and diligently practiced sleight-of-hand and magic tricks, complete with puffs of colored chemical smoke that he had learned from Professor Griscom back in New York. King rehearsed his "speciality," licking irons. The musicians Woodward and Wilbur gave several concerts to raise money and which "whenever given gave the audience general satisfaction." Scudder presumably practiced his poses.

Needing more paints, brushes and canvas, Banvard traveled by stage, being "half jolted to death" in the process, to Mount Vernon on the

Ohio River, where he took the steamboat *Hesione* to Louisville. While there he ran across George Blanchard, former owner of New York's flourishing Chatham Street Amphitheater. Blanchard's spectacular New York equestrian extravaganzas had eventually bankrupted him, and now, down on his luck and trying to improve his lot on the frontier, he operated a clothing store. Banvard purchased what remained of Blanchard's New York theatrical wardrobe and headed back to New Harmony.

The actors' stay in New Harmony wasn't all work. It was a lively and culturally-rich town, unique in American history, and the troupe actively participated in town picnics, dances and what Banvard called "merrymaking." Eventually the outgoing and handsome young entrepreneur became "acquainted with nearly all the people in the town," including Rosiley Fearing, a member of the New Harmony Dramatic Society and who "possessed considerable stage talent." David and William Owen, Robert Owen's sons, had remained behind after the collapse of the commune. David, who worked as chief of the national U.S. Geological Survey headquartered in New Harmony, gave several lectures a week in natural philosophy and Banvard eagerly attended them all. William Owen founded the Thespian Society, later named the New Harmony Dramatic Society. A refurbished Rappite dormitory served as the town's theatre and the Society presented regular seasons of drama for a hundred years, including among its recording secretaries the painter and naturalist John James Audubon ("Minutes New Harmony").

Early one morning Banvard found a sign nailed to the hotel entrance which accused him of mouthing "villainous and obscene epithets." The sign's author, a young lawyer named Barclay, had been Rosiley Fearing's steady escort before Banvard arrived in town. Banvard soon learned the jealous lawyer's identity and tacked up a "humorous and sarcastic rejoinder" below the original sign. Barclay, he wrote, had "reflected on the character of certain estimable young ladies of New Harmony, and if he was not careful he might get a horse whipping." But Banvard wasn't taking any chances. That afternoon, Scudder, the "living statue," gave the young artist "scientific" boxing lessons down on the riverbank. Sure enough, as Banvard walked out of the hotel the next morning, Barclay attacked him. Pinned helplessly between a sign post and a cattle post, Banvard managed to struggle free and, thanks to Scudder's lessons, thoroughly pummeled his rival. Barclay, "amidst the derisive shouts of the spectators," fled into the hotel. A couple of hours later he left by stagecoach for Mt. Carmel, Illinois, never, Banvard claimed, to return to New Harmony. Rosiley's reaction to this violent incident in an otherwise peaceful community is unrecorded.

The company pushed off from New Harmony at two o'clock on the afternoon of December 18, 1834. The first night out they discovered an embarrassing oversight—no one had thought to bring along any bedding! They hastily made a large makeshift bed by throwing together coats, costumes and an old coverlet into the middle of the boat. But the floorboards were so warped and inverted that each person slept in what amounted to a narrow, splintered gutter. When one of the actors rolled over in the night, he pulled the covers off everyone else. Learning to lie perfectly still and adding a blanket or two, the troupe slept in this manner for the entire voyage to New Orleans.

Apparently no evidence survives concerning the details of the rest of the voyage, but the theatrical-retail enterprise must have been successful because Banvard, Scudder, King, and Lowe returned to New Harmony in the summer of 1835 and launched a second theatrical season. The four original members were joined by three more actors—Mr. King, Mr. Karns, and a Mr. Harris. Shortly thereafter, James Bennett and his wife, young newlyweds and actors in the New Harmony Dramatic Society, and W.O. Cox, another local citizen, "good in tragedy and comedy...[who] could dance the Fisher's Hornpipe," and stage manager for the Thespian Society signed up as well (Cox). Versatility was a virtue in frontier theatre.

This second and more ambitious season featured a much larger boat with a completely decked over auditorium and, no longer content to sell groceries, Banvard planned full-scale theatrical productions, including Shakespeare.[6] Despite his grandiose schemes, this second expedition, through illness, lack of money and a capricious river, turned out to be a downright disaster.

The first problem arose when Banvard contracted ague, a common but dangerous frontier malarial disease. He painted once again in the dining room of the New Harmony Hotel and he was especially proud of his drop curtain, "much admired" by New Harmony citizens, which displayed an "architectural Florentine view with an open colonnade receding in perspective." But his illness, accompanied by its violent cycle of fevers and chills, prevented him from painting any other scenery. He decided to finish his work out on the river. Then the company ran out of money before the floating theatre was properly outfitted. They missed their original summer launching date and by late autumn they still had no food, bedding, supplies, or money for finishing the construction of the boat. Banvard decided before leaving New Harmony to give an "entertainment" on board to raise money for three days of provisions and then use the first night's receipts down river to lay in more provisions and to finish modifications to the boat.

On a clear 1835 autumn afternoon, the nine men and one woman launched their floating theatre into the river, hoping to make the meandering 30-mile journey to the mouth of the Wabash and into the Ohio in three days. Once again the bedding was inadequate. They had three mattresses, one of which was allotted to Banvard because of his illness, and the company slept that first unseasonably cool night on the rough, unplaned seats of the auditorium.

Constant nineteenth-century attempts to keep the Wabash River open to navigation failed as the river stubbornly resisted all efforts to control it. Congested with snags, large trees called "sawyers," sand bars, rocks, and hazardous bends, the waterway was one long giant obstacle course that challenged even the best river pilots. At sunrise on their second morning out, the entertainers found the river's water level dangerously low. They put the craft afloat, but it quickly grounded on a sand bar. Straining with levers and rails, the troupe managed to pry the floating theatre loose, but it grounded *five* more times that day. The next morning a fierce headwind prevented them from drifting at all, and they anchored to the shore for the entire day next to Bone Bank Bar, an eerie place where river erosion had exposed the skeletons of an ancient Indian burial mound. Banvard left the boat and "lay on the soft sand of the bar," he would write years later in the third person, "which he found a more comfortable couch than the hard planks of the boat. His head burning with fever, and his limbs aching with pain, he looked at these gloomy relics of an antediluvian race, and felt as though his bones would soon be laid with them" ([John Banvard], "John Banvard's Great Picture" 511). In the evening the desperately ill youth was forced to listen to his fellow performers rehearse John Howard Payne's enduringly popular tune "Home, Sweet Home," a situation he found "not at all edifying."

The next day the wind died down, but the boat soon grounded on a rocky bar, and it was late afternoon before they managed to free it. The fourth day they made even less progress. Banvard had planned on reaching the Ohio in three days, but the floating theatre had traveled less than one-third the necessary distance, and the last of their provisions, a rasher of bacon and a few boiled potatoes, gone. On the fifth day the now frantic rivermen had entangled the boat amongst a series of large boulders, when there suddenly appeared on the Illinois side of the bank an old hunter who, heeding their cries for help, offered to lead them through some now visible and treacherous rapids ahead—for $5. Lowe, whose previous season's $3,000 must have seemed a fortune to him now, had exactly $5 left. It was all that remained of the company's capital funds. Prodded by the constant urging of the old hunter to "give it to her hard, boys, give it to her hard," the actors struggled furiously against the rapids with their long rails. On the evening of the sixth day of the voyage, the exhausted troupe and its embattled showboat reached the Ohio.

Euphoria at reaching the Ohio soon faded. Banvard's condition progressively worsened, no food was on board, and the rest of the company came down with the dreaded malaria. Outside Old Shawneetown, Illinois, the hapless actors, now facing the real threat of starvation, picked rotting pawpaws out of the river and ate them raw. A curious crowd gathered on the riverbank to watch this strange sight, and when a man rowed out in a canoe to investigate, the troupe went back to shore with him for food. Banvard, too ill to move from his mattress, gave the actor Harris his last 25 cents to buy some quinine, probably "Dr. Sappington's Anti-Fever Pills," the standard frontier malaria remedy. Harris instead spent the night carousing and drinking in Old Shawneetown, a village with a rough reputation, and returned to the boat in the early hours of the morning to inform Banvard that he had spent the 25 cents on liquor. He then unceremoniously dumped Banvard off his coveted mattress, telling the miserable painter that he was tired of sleeping on hard benches and that Banvard had had the luxury of a mattress ever since they left New Harmony.

This company, unlike the 1834 troupe, had no written contract for sharing work, duties and profits. Exhausted from their labors on the Wabash, sick with malarial fever, and once again hungry, tempers flared. They soon fell to arguing over the merest slight and occasionally fistfights broke out. Off Golconda, Illinois, some 30 river miles below Old Shawneetown, three of the actors were shaking so badly from fever they had difficulty finishing the night's performance. One of them, Kemble, left the stage to vomit over the side guard for several minutes, leaving the other actors to improvise Shakespeare during his absence. But they couldn't stop the show—"It was play or starve," Banvard later lamented, "as there were no provisions on the boat and the night's receipts was [sic] depended on to procure supper."

Eventually the other actors fell too ill to work, while Banvard himself gradually recovered. He bailed water out of the the now badly leaking floating theatre, trudged along the shoreline searching for farms that might provide some milk for the company, tended as best he could to the sick, and washed all the clothes by dragging them in the water behind the boat. At Paducah, Kentucky, Banvard, while wandering along the waterfront begging for food, met John Betts, a local businessman and fledgling theatre owner. Betts went out to the boat, liked what he saw of Banvard's scenic paintings, and, taking pity on the young man before him, who by now was a "regular living skeleton," offered him a job in a new theatre he was constructing. It was a generous and risky act on Betts's part. As the head of Paducah's board of health (Robertson 111) he would have been in charge of keeping sick people out of the town, not, as he eventually did, taking them into his home.

Betts's interest in theatre came from his marriage to an English actress, Josephine Betts. Once he decided to start up a theatre in Paducah, he quickly put together a competent little company that included Mrs. Betts; her son from a previous marriage, Thomas Mitchell; and her two sisters Mrs. Hallam and Rachel Stannard. The three sisters had come to Kentucky in a roundabout way that furnishes an insight into the peripatetic life of the frontier actor. In 1826 in Philadelphia, English actor John Hallam asked his boss, theatre manager Joseph Cowell (See Chapter 3), for a leave of absence to go back to England and find a wife. Cowell jokingly gave his permission on the condition that if he found any talented actors who were willing to work for £3 a week, we was to bring them back with him. Hallam returned with the new Mrs. Hallam and her two sisters, a brother-in-law, and a nephew. "The rest of the family," Cowell noted dryly, "couldn't come, I suppose." Mrs. Betts, who had "a very pretty face and a broad Lincolnshire accent," was widowed soon after her arrival in America. Cowell, whether out of sympathy or the need for character actresses, offered her double salary to play old women (Cowell 80, 81). She made her New York debut in *The Wandering Boys* at the Lafayette Theatre on January 6, 1829 (Odell III, 469). It was there that John Betts met her and proposed. They returned to Paducah and opened their theatre. Mrs. Betts's sister Rachel Stannard (b. 1800) joined them from St. Louis where in July 1835 she had played Ophelia opposite the prominent frontier actor Charles K. Mason at Noah Ludlow's Salt House Theatre (Carson 149-50). Little Thomas Mitchell played the children's parts, an elderly Louisville actor named King played the old man roles, and several Paducah amateurs rounded out the troupe.

The Betts family took Banvard into their home and helped him recover from the devastating effects of his illness and labors. In return for medicine, room, board, and a small salary, Banvard provided Betts's theatre with scenery and interior decorations. He sold his interest in the showboat to Lowe for $90, a sum that Lowe, naturally, didn't have, took up residence in the Betts household, and never saw any of the members of showboat troupe again.

The floating theatre continued down the Mississippi River until it reached the tiny settlement of Randolph, Tennessee, where the expedition met a sudden and grim denouement. It began when W.O. Cox accused Lowe of withholding his share of the meager profits and he had the boat attached by a local constable for "unpaid wages." An altercation broke out, during which Lowe sustained severe wounds from a Bowie knife. When the constable came aboard the floating theatre to see what the commotion was all about, he fell through the stage trap door, broke his neck, and died. Now fugitives, the ill-fated troupe quickly dispersed. The unfortunate Bennetts—who knows what went through the mind of poor Mrs. Bennett, the only woman aboard, so far away from home and family—eventually made their way back home to New Harmony, as did W.O. Cox. Scudder, the "personification of motionless marble," gave up show business altogether and eventually settled in Equality, Illinois, where for several years he ran a notorious saloon (Cox). The other performers disappeared without a trace, apparently swallowed up, like so many itinerant performers before and after them, by the vast wilderness of the Western river systems from which they came. Banvard, however, recovered, and as we shall see, left showboats for another kind of touring entertainment. He would go on to produce the world's largest painting and amass a fortune while launching the moving panorama movement in America.

Chapter 2
William Henry Lane, "Master Juba":
The Man Who Invented Tap Dance

Not all hardships encountered by theatrical and paratheatrical entertainers occurred on the frontier. Life for the itinerant variety artist was hard in the city, too. What follows is a particularly instructive urban American story about a man who grew up in the most squalid circumstances, who battled an inherently racist collection of performers to develop his own deeply influential art form, and who, in the end, died at an early age, probably from malnutrition and overwork. He was an African-American named William Henry Lane (1828?-1852) and, unique for his time, he worked as a burnt-cork blackfaced minstrel before exclusively white audiences.

The black minstrel show, that curious American phenomonen in which white actors donned black faces and parodied the African-American slave experience, was this country's most popular form of theatrical entertainment in the nineteenth century. One-hundred and fifty years later, the minstrel show unfortunately remains the "only distinctively American contribution to theatre" (Wittke 3). In the midst of this phenomonen, a cultural travesty that cannot but offend the modern sensibility, William Henry Lane's name should tower above all others. Now generally forgotten, his life's work demonstrates remarkable accomplishment in the face of overwhelming odds. Performing as "Master Juba," this dancer and singer enjoyed a meteoric career between 1845 and 1850, forging in the process the steps, techniques and routines that are now called the "tap dance." William Henry Lane, says dance historian Marian Hannah Winter, whose work on Lane is a major source for this essay, was the "most influential single performer of nineteenth-century American dance" (Winter 20).

Black-faced white performers were fairly common on the legitimate stage during the 1820s and 1830s, and several actors—J.W. Sweeney, Bob Farrell, who performed under the stage name "Zip Coon," George

Washington Dixon, among others—earned their professional reputations in single acts performing "alleged Negro songs and dances in circuses and between the acts of plays" (Toll, *Blacking Up* 27).[1] While the notion of the minstrel troupe evolved in urban New York City popular theatres, its progenitor was Thomas Dartmouth Rice (1808-1860), who in 1828, while working as a bit player and stagehand in Samuel Drake's Louisville Theatre company, introduced in blackface during an interval of a performance of *The Rifle* the eccentric song and dance "Jim Crow," which he claimed he copied from a slave on the Louisville docks and whose title carries a much different connotation in modern America (Wittke 33). The popularity of "Jim Crow" spread like wildfire, and series of entertainments based on white perceptions, or at least expectations, of the black slave experience became all the rage in America and England. By the mid-1840s, a typical minstrel program, referred to as "Ethiopian opera," or more commonly, "nigger minstrelsy," featured a semi-circle of at least eight performers as its centerpiece and consisted of mock Shakespeare soliloquies, political "stump" speeches, rapid-fire and often absurd jokes, instrumental music, dancing, and singing.

The musical selections, at least in the early years, emphasized the slave family unit and were filled with sentimental deaths, slave auctions, and emotional songs about "mother," with a mixture of raucous and fast-paced jingles thrown in for variety. Written mostly by Northern white composers such as Stephen Foster and based on simple English and Irish folk melodies, these songs became the most popular music of the day and tunes like "Camptown Races," "Jeannie with the Light Brown Hair," and "Oh, Susannah" are an ingrained part of our popular culture. One of the handful of black composers was James Bland (1854-1911), who counted among his 700 published songs "Carry Me Back to Old Virginny" and "Dem Golden Slippers." [2]

With its racially insulting humor and its undeniably infectious energy, the minstrel show perpetuated for nearly 75 years the worst racial myths and stereotypes, invariably portraying African-Americans as wide-grinned, inferior, lazy, stupid, and watermelon-eating innocents. The favorite theatregoing activity of mass white audiences, minstrelsy counted among its fans the most prominent individuals of the day, including Queen Victoria and Abraham Lincoln, whose favorite song was the minstrel tune "Dixie."

Fig. 2. William Henry Lane. Under the stage name Master Juba, this innovative and influential performer introduced audiences to the tap dance. From a sketch in the August 5, 1848 edition of the *Illustrated London News. Author's Collection.*

26 "It Was Play or Starve"

The minstrel show's enduring attraction for white audiences, as theatre historian Robert C. Toll points out in his studies of the subject, sprang from a new "common man's culture" that by mid-century was white, demanding, hungry for novel entertainment, and desperate to establish its racial superiority. Later, after the Civil War, when white America "made crucial decisions about the rights and status of black people," the minstrel show dominated the American entertainment scene because of "deepseated racial and sociological reasons" ("Showbiz in Blackface" 170). Before Toll, white theatre scholars either ignored the sociological implications of or patronized the human characters in the minstrel show. Typical was Carl Wittke, whose *Tambo and Bones* (1930) was considered until recently the standard minstrel history, who commented that "the Negro has a real sense of rhythm" and who said that his own book on the subject was the result of "happy memories of the burnt cork semi-circle gathered during barnstorming student days." His work, intended as a "serious contribution to American social history," attempted to demonstrate that "from the pathos and humor of the Negroes, their superstitions and their religious fervor, their plaintive and their hilarious melodies, their peculiarities of manner, dress and speech, the white minstrel built his performance" (Wittke 3, vii, 7). Professional minstrelsy and blackface didn't go away—BBC television in England employed the Kentucky Minstrels, a white troupe in blackface, well into the 1960s,[3] while Americans in the 1950s watched Eddie Cantor in blackface on CBS television's "The Ed Sullivan Show" and in the 1990s saw blackfaced actors employing plantation dialects on the imported English television series "The Benny Hill Show."

Not much is known about William Henry Lane. We do not know, for instance, where or when he was born. One of his contemporaries said that he was a free-born black from Providence, Rhode Island, and several publicity posters list that as his city of origin. A reasonable guess would be that he was born between 1825 and 1828 (Leavitt 91; Haskins 24; Winter 31). What is known, however, is that he grew up in the notorious Five Points section of lower Manhattan.

Five Points, infamous for its squalor and unrelenting poverty, was described in 1842 by a visiting Charles Dickens as "reeking everywhere with dirt and filth...debauchery has made the very houses prematurely old [and] poverty, wretchedness and vice are rife" (107). City officials discovered that one small dilapidated building known as the "Old

Brewery" housed over 1,000 people before it was torn down in 1852 (Spann 68). In the midst of "lanes and alleys paved with mud knee deep" and "hideous tenements," wrote Dickens, lay row on row of saloons, brothels and gaming houses (109). Five Points was also home to two of America's lowest underclasses— recent Irish immigrants and free-born African-Americans. It was here in the saloons and dance halls that afforded the only escapist entertainment for these two groups, thrown together in an uneasy alliance, that blacks adapted traditional Irish clog and jig dances and fused them with traditional African forms.

Lane's teacher during his youth was reputed to be neighborhood legend Uncle Jim Lowe, an innovative and energetic dancer who worked in saloons, dances halls and other performance spaces outside regular theatres (Winter 31). Lane's own contribution to dance history, apparently formulated by the age of fourteen, was to adapt an African dance called *giouba* to the traditional Irish jig-and-reel. The resulting "Juba" dance, variations of which existed before Lane and traces of which still can be found anywhere in the Western Hemisphere that had early African settlements, became a series of rapid toe-heel syncopations with little or no musical accompaniment (Jones 37-40; Courlander 190-92). Lane also apparently developed the technique of crossing and uncrossing his hands against his moving kneecaps—a movement that became an integral part of the 1920s popular dance, the Charleston (Winter 30). Lane and his many later imitators based their dances on a single element—rhythm. The feet became percussive musical instruments replacing the drum, castanets, bones, and tambourine. Arm movements were kept to a minimum and attention was focused on the intricacies and rapidity of carefully and cleanly delineated toe-and-heel dance steps.[4] Sometime between 1840 and 1842, through Lane's innovations and his mastery of the form, the modern tap dance was born.

In the only surviving portrait of Lane, an August 5, 1848 *Illustrated London News* woodcut, we see that he wears a frock coat, hands stuck deep in his pockets. Peering downwards, he concentrates on his footwork and apparently on the *sound* of his dance. He, like his fellow white minstrels, wears burnt-cork facial make-up. Charles Dickens's 1842 Five Points visit provides us with our one indelible portrait of the young William Henry Lane at work. It is quoted at length here because, as an eyewitness account by a master journalist, it captures the electrifying energy and effect of Lane's dance on an audience. Dickens, led by two policemen up the crumbling stairway of a tenement, stumbled into a dimly lit dance hall filled with black and Irish revelers. "The corpulent black fiddler," Dickens wrote, "and his friend who plays the tambourine, stamp upon the boarding of the small raised orchestra in which they sit, and play a lively measure." Then

> Five or six couples come upon the floor, marshalled by a lively young Negro, who is the wit of the assembly, and the greatest dancer known...Among the dancers are two young mulatto girls, with large, black, drooping eyes, and headgear after the fashion of the hostess, who are as shy or feign to be, as though they had never danced before, and so look down before the visitors, that their partners can see nothing but the long fringed lashes.
>
> But the dance commences. Every gentleman sets as long as he likes to the opposite lady and the lady to his, and all are so long about it that the sport begins to languish, when suddenly the lively hero dashes in to the rescue. Instantly the fiddler grins, and goes at it tooth and nail; there is new energy in the dances; new smiles in the landlady; new confidence in the landlord; new brightness in the very candle. Single shuffle, double shuffle, cut and cross cut; snapping his fingers, rolling his eyes, turning in his knees, presenting the backs of his legs in front, spinning about on his toes and heels like nothing but the man's fingers on the tambourine; dancing with two left legs, two right legs, two wooden legs, two wire legs, two spring legs—all sorts of legs and no legs— what is this to him? And in what walk of life, or dance of life, does man ever get such stimulating applause as thunders about him, when, having danced his partner off her feet, and himself too, he finishes by leaping gloriously on the bar-counter and [calls] for something to drink. (109-111)

William Henry Lane, somewhere around 14 years old when Dickens saw him perform, soon became famous. He drew the attention of New Yorkers when he performed at Pete Williams's dance hall in Orange Street. His act consisted of imitating perfectly all the leading dancers of the day and then, when the master of ceremonies commanded "Now, Master Juba, show your own jig," Lane would go into his own tap dance, displaying "not only...wonderful and unique execution, but also...unsurpassed grace and endurance." This mimicking of lesser dancers would become one of his professional trademarks, all the more emphasizing the skill and artistry of his own African-American inspired dancing. But he was not only a skilled dancer; he also possessed a first-rate tenor voice and was a "tambourine virtuoso" (Winter 31).

In 1845, now around 17 years old and acknowledged as the greatest dancer in America, Lane toured with three white musicians, earning in the process a significant place in the history of American show business as the only black to receive top billing in regular theatres between the great tragedian Ira Aldridge in the 1820s and the end of the Civil War. This was truly an extraordinary achievement in the face of the entertainment industry's overwhelming racism. Lane and the violin-playing minstrel dwarf Thomas Dilward, known as "Japanese Tommy" and generally considered a sideshow entertainer, may have been the only blacks performing on stages with white companies during this period (Odell, VIII, 385; Brown *History of the American Stage* 312).[5]

Lane and his three white partners—T. Fluter (banjo), J.T. Brown (tambourine), Amidon L. Thayer (singer)—performed a fast-paced, six-part variety show of music, song, and dance. J.T. Brown may be Joe Brown (d. 1883), himself a prominent minstrel dancer in the late 1860s and winner of a "silver belt" in challenge competition. Amidon Thayer (1823-1864), then 22 years old, would go on to be a highly successful minstrel troupe manager (Toll 197). A surviving playbill of the small troupe gives us our earliest look at Lane's repertoire.[6] A chorus was listed in the program, but, in the tradition of itinerant entertainers, it probably consisted of the other three partners who weren't singing solo at the time. Lane sat out Part I as Brown, Fluter and Thayer sang "Life by de Gallery Fire," Town of Tuscalore" and "Who dat knocking at de door" respectively. Part II consisted entirely of Lane doing his "Statue Dance." In Part III, the four members all sang popular ballads and upbeat tunes: Thayer-"I Must go to Richmond," Brown-"Old Gal come to de garden gate," Lane -"Juliana Johnson," and Thayer-"Forty five miles." J.T. Brown next played a "solo on the Tambourine," imitating "where the locomotive runs off the track and bursts the Boiler, also the rattling of Cannon in the distance...his imitations of a celebrated French Drummer...his Grist Mill grindings showing the power of steam, (of course) and the rattling of a Cotton mill and machinery. Language cannot convey any idea of his brilliant rapidity of execution on his Tambourine." After more songs—Thayer-"Early in de morning," Lane-"Farewell Ladies," Brown-"Lynchburg Town"—and T. Fluter's "Solo on the Banjo," the program was brought to a conclusion by Lane's extraordinary talents:

Imitation Dance, by Mast. Juba, in which he will give correct Imitation Dances of all the principal Ethiopian Dancers in the United States. After which he will give an imitation of himself—and then you will see the vast difference between those that have heretofore attempted dancing and the WONDERFUL YOUNG MAN. Names of the Persons Imitated:

1. Richard Pelham. New York.
2. Mr. Francis Brower. New York.
3. Mr. John Daniels. Buffalo.
4. Mr. John Smith. Albany.
5. Mr. James Stanford. Philadelphia.
6. Mr. Frank Diamond. Troy.
7. Master John Diamond. New York.

Lane achieved his greatest recognition as the result of a string of challenge matches against the best minstrel dancers of the day. His opponents included the dancers listed in the 1845 playbill, all of whom headed their own successful minstrel troupes. His greatest rival and most formidable opponent, however, was "Master" John Diamond (1823-1857), a short, alcoholic, foul-tempered man who was known for the precision of his step execution. Diamond, also a teenaged phenomenon, was at one time managed by none other than P.T. Barnum himself, and, according to Noah Ludlow, who booked him for an engagement in New Orleans when he was 16 years old, "could twist his feet and legs, while dancing, into more fantastic forms than I ever witnessed before or since in any human being" (Ludlow 533). But Lane handily defeated all comers in challenge matches, including Diamond twice in legendary dance marathons for a $500 prize at New York's Chatham Theatre and again at the Bowery Theatre. All the challengers, all the judges, and, in matches taking place at regular theatres, all the audiences were white (Stearns 44).

These challenge matches were highly organized affairs and they lasted well into the twentieth century, where show business legend has it that Fred Astaire and Bill "Bojangles" Robinson engaged in after hours contests at a Broadway theatre (Stearns 186). In Lane's time, three judges were present. A style judge sat in the orchestra pit facing the dancers, a time judge sat stage right where the contestants made their entrance, and an execution judge sat *underneath* the stage, checking with paper and pencil missed taps and faulty steps. One dancer would execute his dance and then his opponent would mimic as precisely as possible the same steps. Then they reversed the order. Prizes were awarded on points. This challenge form, by the way, remains a fixture in the standard tap dance repertoire (Gilbert, 203; Engle 13-20).

Lane moved out of the saloons and into regular theatres by signing with the Georgia Champion Minstrels and touring New England. His publicity posters noted his triumphs over Diamond and stated, "No conception can be formed of all the variety of beautiful and intricate steps exhibited by him with ease. You must see to believe." "Beautiful," notes Marian Hannah Winter, was a word seldom used to describe the often grotesque bendings and contortions that passed for white minstrel dancing (Winter 34).

In January 1848, his most successful year as a performer, he was at New York's Pinteux's Saloon, where he appeared as a solo artist with Pete Morris (b. 1821), a comic singer; Cecilia Blanchard, who performed monologues; and Jeanie Reynoldson (d. 1869), a singer. During the first week of February he was engaged by Charles White (1821-1891) for his White's Negro Minstrels at the Melodeon Theatre, 53 Bowery Street, which, said the *New York Herald*, "was crowded every night to see Master Juba's dancing feats" (Odell V, 397, 400).

Sometime during the summer of 1848, Lane left White's Negro Minstrels and traveled to London where he joined up with the most successful minstrel troupe to date, Pell's Ethiopian Serenaders. His impact was immediate and dramatic. Performing at Vauxhall Gardens, a popular variety theatre that attracted every stratum of London society, he astounded audiences and critics alike with his tap dancing. British reviewers struggled to find an adequate vocabulary to describe what it was that he did. His laugh alone, said one, was "like the continuous humming sound of nature...It enters your heart and you laugh sympathetically—it creeps into your ear, and clings to it." The same critic said he'd never seen such a combination of

Mobility of muscles, such flexibility of joints, such boundings, such slidings, such gyrations, such toes and heelings, such backwardings and forwardings, such posturing, such firmness of foot, such elasticity of tendon, such mutation of movement, such vigor, such variety, such natural grace, such powers of endurance.

Another wondered "how could he tie his legs into such knots and fling them about so recklessly, or make his feet twinkle until you lost sight of them altogether in his energy?" At a private performance at Vauxhall Gardens, a visitor, who noted that Lane was "only in his seventeenth year," thought,

> The dancing of Juba exceeded anything ever witnessed in Europe. The style as well as the execution is unlike anything ever seen in this country. The manner in which he beats time with his feet, and the extraordinary command he possesses over them, can only be believed by those who have been present at his exhibition. Scarcely less singular is the rapidity with which he sings one of his favorite songs.

It was announced that Juba had been summoned for a command performance at Buckingham Palace, but no record of such an event survives. Later Pell's Ethiopians toured the provinces and enjoyed a particularly successful engagement in Liverpool (Winter 35-7).

Then in London in 1852, still in his late 20s, Lane inexplicably died. The British Public Records Office and the U.S. State Department have no record of a death certificate for Lane, and the reasons for his death, like the events of his personal life and the source of his extraordinary talent, remain a mystery. T. Allston Brown, an acid-tongued contemporary of Lane's, stated that "success proved too much for him. He married too late (and a white woman besides) and died early and miserable" (Brown, "The Origin of Minstrelsy"). Few other contemporary performers made mention of him, whether out of ingrained racism, professional jealousy or both, we'll never know. Thomas Dartmouth Rice, the man who started the whole minstrel phenomonen, grudgingly acknowledged that Lane was "considered the greatest dancer in his line" and that he died. Period. Whatever the pressures of success or of an interracial marriage in a deeply segregated society, Lane's early death probably resulted from something as simple and as pathetic as overwork. From his earliest youth until 1852, Lane performed day and night in a variety of houses and theatres. During most of his life he literally performed for his supper. An on-the-house meal in Five Points during his youth consisted of a plate of fried eels and a tankard of ale (Winter 37), hardly a balanced diet both for his strenuous dancing routines and for the frequency with which he performed them.

Lane's premature death robbed the minstrel industry of its only black star and destroyed any pretense that white American minstrelsy contained authentic elements of African-American culture. Late in the nineteenth century when black entertainers were finally allowed to perform for mass white audiences, they were forced to work as—what else?—minstrels. Dozens of black minstrel troupes toured the Northern United States during the last quarter of the nineteenth century. And despite energy, extraordinary talent and musical innovation, troupes— Robert C. Toll counts at least 28 of them during the 1870s—wore blackface, imitated *white* minstrels, adopted the formats and conventions of white troupes, and performed before white audiences. These pioneers, forced by economics and a racially-biased culture to adhere to the minstrel show format, nevertheless were able in some instances to introduce modifications to the black caricatures fostered by their white predecessors. For all the opportunities allowed black performers after the Civil War and the ability of black troupes to establish a foothold in American show business, the period of the minstrel show remains one America's great artistic and social tragedies (Toll 195-223; Haskins 34-53; Armstead-Johnson 77-86).[7]

But William Henry Lane was, by all accounts, his own person and he remained true to his urban African-American roots. He did perform in blackface. But he didn't join in any of the lamentable stump speeches, he didn't engage in invented "plantation" dialect, and he didn't present himself as a figure of ridicule. Instead, he danced and sang, and through the sheer force of his talent and creative genius and in the face of overwhelming odds, singlehandedly imposed the black tradition on American dance. His legacy is firm and unchallenged. Dancers, white and black, who came after him—men such as Richard M. Carroll (1831-1899?), a protegé of Diamond's who adopted Lane's routines instead, and Dave Reed (1830-1906)—kept his steps, and in doing so, kept "in touch with the integrity of Negro source material" in show business (Winter 46). William Henry Lane's tap dances outlived minstrelsy, thrived on vaudeville and variety show stages and eventually became an imbedded part of American popular culture, permanently divorced from the tawdry arena of the minstrel show that became Lane's only vehicle for widespread recognition in a racist society.

Chapter 3
The "Great Three-Mile" Painting

Another unique entertainment form that captured the imagination of nineteenth-century mass audiences was the panorama show, the exhibition of huge paintings on practically any subject one could imagine. Panoramas gripped both the American and British public alike as no popular art form before it and the craze was so widespread it has been dubbed "panoramania." As a forerunner of the cinematic newsreel, these paintings offered pictorially transmitted information on history, current events, religion, travel—any large-scale subject whose comprehension could be boosted by the moving image. In his study of American frontier panorama entertainments, Joseph Schick reflects, "Contemporary news events at home and abroad became vivid actualities. In an age devoid of our ready methods of picture reproduction, the panorama served as an oasis in the desert of the printed page" (Schick, *Early Theatre in Eastern Iowa* 136). While in France, the master artist David took his students to a Daguerre exhibit and was overheard to murmur, "Really, one has to come here to study Nature" (Gernsheim 6).

Scottish portraitist Robert Barker (1739-1806) is credited with the "invention" of the panorama. He originally came up with an idea for painting an entirely circular landscape, a full 360°, one which, as the viewer stood at the center of the work, would give the illusion of reality. But he couldn't make it work. His early sketches, which relied on the basic principles of single-point perspective developed by Renaissance artists, only worked at eye level; the rest of the drawings above or below eye level were severely distorted. Through trial and error, and with the help of his 12-year-old son, he solved this vexing puzzle "by inventing a system of curved lines that would neutralize the distortion created by a concave surface" (Altick 129).[1] He applied for a patent in Edinburgh in 1787, produced painted views of that city and the surrounding area and put them on public display. In 1792, under the patronage of influential artists like Benjamin West (1738-1829) and Joshua Reynolds (1723-92), he constructed a circular building in London's Leicester Square and exhibited a series of paintings titled "English fleet anchored between Portsmouth and the Isle of Wight." American Robert Fulton (1765-1815), studying under West in London, saw Barker's work and was intrigued by the financial potential of the panorama form. He received "exclusive rights" to display panoramas in Paris, but, while this painting genre later became a Parisian craze, he couldn't work things out financially. He sold his rights to entrepreneur/artist James Thayer, returned to America, and devoted his energies to building the first working steamboat.

These early panoramic paintings were based on a simple premise: seated in the center of the circular, unframed painting, a spectator felt a part of the environment of the work, that he or she "was participating in the astonishing illusion of reality in the depicted scene" (Gernsheims 3). Guides led viewers through a dark tunnel into a circular central room of the specially-constructed panorama building. Chairs, 150 in Thayer's first hall, were placed in the center as equidistant from the painting as possible. The illumination came from above the ceiling and behind it, so the viewer saw no ceiling or framing device (McDermott 5).

Parisian L.J.M. Daguerre (1789-1851), the inventor of photography, helped alter the panoramic form in 1821 when he assisted in the invention of the diorama. Rendered on transparent linen, dioramas were large paintings that used cut-outs in the canvas, moving machinery parts and changing lighting, fog and smoke for special, often spectacular, effects. Daguerre's exhibition of "The Interior of Trinity Chapel, Canterbury Cathedral," for example, was so realistic that one elderly patron asked for the artist's assistance to "be conducted down the [painted] steps to walk" into the cathedral (Gernsheims 3).

The next development in this unusual art form was the moving panorama, a painting that passed by the spectator as it slowly unwound from a tall cylinder. The improvement was significant. Formerly static, a panorama's only restriction on length was now the size of the roller that held it.

Panoramas got off to a slow start in America. John Vanderlyn (1775-1852) in 1818 built a large rotunda in New York to house his painting of Versailles, but the movement lagged overall because landscapes were of less interest to American popular taste than portraits and sentimental domestic scenes. By the late 1830s, however, inspired by the large landscapes of Thomas Cole (1801-1848) and the Hudson River School, native American artists began adopting the panoramic form. Theatrical scene painters, because of their speed, skill at background detail, and mastery of both perspective and large-scale painting techniques, emerged as the most successful in the trade. They also possessed knowledge of theatrical mechanics, an essential part of the moving panorama show. The panorama and diorama exhibitions also began to reflect an emerging nationalism and as the 1800s wore on, foreign subject matter—Biblical themes, views of Egypt, Venice, Moscow, and Paris, etc.—gave way to American themes with titles like "Bunker Hill," "American Fleet Against Tripoli," "A Trip to Niagara," "A Trip up the Hudson River," "Bullard's Panorama of New York City," "Mammoth Cave in Kentucky."

The exhibition of these panoramas, both in England and America, developed into a theatrical event. Lectures, musical accompaniment, darkened halls, special lighting effects, and heavy publicity resulted in a wholly new entertainment form. By the late 1840s, following dozens of spectacular London panorama and diorama shows and increasing audience interest in America, the stage was set for the greatest panoramist of all, the "doyen of the trade" (Altick 204). His name was John Banvard, the unfortunate showboat entrepreneur in Chapter 1.

After Banvard left the Betts Family troupe in 1835, he travelled the Cumberland, Missouri, Ohio, and Mississippi rivers dabbling in portraiture, decorating public buildings and displaying his modest landscapes. Occasionally he found work in a theatre. It was in St. Louis, sharing a bill with Miss Hayden, the "far-famed American Sybil," that he began displaying larger paintings. On April 19, 1841, he announced the presentation of the "terribly terrific spectacle" of the "INFERNAL REGIONS, nearly 100 feet in length" plus a "GRAND PANORAMA OF ST. LOUIS." An "infernal regions" diorama had been traveling around the Midwest for years. Created in Cincinnati in the late 1820s by Auguste Hervieu and Hiram Powers (1805-73), the romantic sculptor whose nude work "The Greek Slave" made him a national figure, with the assistance of the visiting Mrs. Trollope, author and mother of novelist Anthony Trollope, this ingenious painting had a little working railroad transporting mechanical sinners to hell. The rails gave off a "galvanic shock when touched by unsuspecting visitors" (McDermott

22; Buley, II, 578). Banvard's work was probably a copy of Hervieu and Powers. The budding showman built his career on imitating works and then making the imitation more profitable than the original.

Seized by the restlessness and hunger for adventure that characterized his nature, Banvard hit upon the idea of painting a moving panorama of the whole Mississippi River from St. Louis to New Orleans. His project eventually would result in the longest painting in history, vast international acclaim for the artist and hundreds of thousands, perhaps millions, of dollars for its creator. Banvard, in the pamphlets that accompanied his Mississippi River Panorama exhibitions, said the idea came to him as a boy and he planned the panorama during his first voyage down the Ohio River to Louisville in 1831: "As he glided along by the beautiful shores, the boy resolved within himself to be an Artist, that he might paint the beauties and sublimities of his native land...His grand object was to produce the largest painting in the world" ("Mr. John Banvard" Banvard File). On another occasion he claimed the idea came from those critics who said "America has not the artists commensurate with the grandeur and extent of her scenery." In a rush of patriotic fervor, Banvard decided to prove them wrong (*Littell's Living Age* 15 Dec. 1847: 511).

His statement that he planned the painting as a boy was undoubtedly a ploy to counter later rivals, all of whom claimed they thought of the idea first. The most likely inspiration for the painting is that Banvard, through his St. Louis experience, discovered that a well-publicized panorama could be a lucrative moneymaking enterprise. For most of his career, like every good showman, he staked his "livelihood on a shrewd perception, if not anticipation, of what the public wanted at a given moment" (Altick 3). Until some disastrous business enterprises later in life, Banvard consistently created entertainment the public was eager to pay for. And the one undisputable talent he possessed as a painter—the ability to work rapidly and accurately—was ideally suited for large-scale paintings.

In the spring of 1842 Banvard bought pencils, brushes and paper and in a small skiff set out on the Missouri River just above St. Louis bound for an epic one-man journey to New Orleans. He sketched as he glided along in the current, putting up by the shore at night. He described the experience in his unpublished holograph autobiography.

The Missouri [illegible] a light pine staff and on a bright sunny morning in

Fig. 3. Banvard making sketches for his panorama on the shores of the Mississippi River. Artist unknown, c. 1849. *Minnesota Historical Society*. Reprinted with permission.

May I pushed off in the rapid current of the river to begin my apparently endless labor. The currents of the Missouri and Mississippi River flow quite rapidly, averaging four to six miles an hour. So I made fair progress along down the stream and began to fill my portfolio with sketches of the river shores. At first it appeared lonesome to me drifting all day in my little boat, but I finally got used to this. Where the scenery was monotonous and uninteresting as much of it is, I would let my skiff drift unattended down the current of nights while I would lie on my hay in the bottom and sleep. The noise of a passing steamer would always awaken me, then I would pull out of his way. (Banvard MS. 6302, BFP)

Banvard's anonymously written pamphlets offered less reverie and more drama.

He would be weeks together without speaking to a human being, having no other company than his rifle, which furnished him with his meat from the game of the woods or the fowl of the river. Several nights during the time, he was compelled to creep from under his skiff, where he slept, and sit all night on a log and breast the pelting storm... During this time he pulled his little skiff more than two thousand miles. The sun the while was so intensively hot, that his skin became so burned that it peeled off the backs of his hands and from his face. His eyes became inflamed by such constant and extraordinary effort. ([John Banvard], *Description* 9-10)

Banvard returned north to Louisville with several sketchpads filled with river views. He acquired a larger boat and made a second trip trading goods down the river, just as he had done on his first New Harmony showboat. He came back to Louisville in 1844, and built a large barn on the outskirts of the city. He worked odd jobs, including the interior decoration of the Louisville Odd Fellow's Hall, to make ends meet (Arrington 212).

In April 1846, an old childhood friend, Lt. Selim Woodworth, son of Samuel Woodworth, minor American writer famous for his poem "The Old Oaken Bucket," passed through Louisville on a military expedition. He found Banvard struggling with *"three miles of canvas!"* and noted that "within the studio all seemed in chaos and confusion."

Here and there were scattered about the floor piles of original sketches, bales of canvas, and heaps of boxes. Paint boxes, jars, and kegs were stowed about without order or arrangement, while along one of the walls several large cases were piled, containing rolls of finished sections of the painting. On the opposite wall was spread a canvas, extending the length of the wall, upon which the artist was then at work. A portion of this canvas was on an upright roller, or drum, standing at one end of the building, and as the artist completes his painting, he thus disposes of it.... The mode of exhibiting it is ingenious, and will require considerable machinery. It will be placed upon upright revolving cylinders and the canvas gradually will pass before the spectator, thus affording the artist the opportunity to explain the whole work. (*Description*, Putnam Edition 4-5)

Woodworth provides the earliest documentation of the size of the "Panorama of the Mississippi, Missouri, and Ohio Rivers." The claim of three miles, while never seriously questioned by either Banvard's public or his rivals, is an exaggeration. Richard Altick, in his study *The Shows of London*, estimated that the canvas would have passed by the spectator at 132 feet a minute to be seen in a two hour performance (Altick 204). Banvard always carefully pointed out that *others called* it three miles of canvas, noting in his publicity that the painting was "extensively known as the Three-Mile Picture." The figure most often given for its length was 1,320 feet (*Holden's Dollar Magazine* New York). Although Banvard later added scenes from the Missouri and Ohio rivers, this latter figure is probably correct. Since the painting was 12 feet high, the total *area* in its original form was 15,840 *square feet*, not three miles in linear measurement. Banvard's "ingenious" machinery for showing the Panorama consisted of a grommeted upper track system that kept the top of the canvas taut and eliminated the sagging problem that plagued previous panorama showmen. His device was sufficiently innovative to be the subject of an admiring article in *Scientific American* ("Banvard's Panorama" 100).

In June 1846, after four years of labor, Banvard rented a hall in Louisville and, in wonderful understatement, advertised "a mile or so" of his painting for public view. The Louisville Gas Company, either because of the complexity of the artist's lighting scheme or because of past experience with unreliable theatre troupes and exhibitors, demanded double the usual installation fee for gas fixtures. The artist traded one of his unnamed inventions to a local scientific society for 50 paid advance tickets, and, without a moment to spare, raised enough cash for his installation fee. On June 29 he announced "Banvard's Grand Moving Panorama of the Mississippi will open at the Apollo Rooms, on Monday Evening, June 29, 1846, and continue every evening till Saturday, July 4." Admission was 50 cents for adults, half price for children and servants. But on opening night, June 29, 1846, not a single soul turned up. Banvard blamed bad weather, the showman's curse. The Louisville *Morning Courier* agreed, remarking, "The business of the Panorama, Theatre, Garden, Ice Creameries, etc., was most essentially done for. It has been some time since we had such a a hard and incessant rain as last night" (Louisville, *Morning Courier* 29 June 1846; *Description*, Putnam Edition 14; *Louisville Democrat*, 29 June 1986; Louisville *Morning Courier* 30 June 1846). Banvard, plucky as ever, went down to the Louisville docks, buttonholed steamboat crewmen and passed out free tickets, hoping that word of mouth would pull in customers. It worked so well that by the end of the week he was forced to turn customers away. The exhibition run was extended. The panorama was such a success that several surrounding towns organized steamboat excursions to see the exhibition and "for a solid month he did great business" (Robinson 3). By now Banvard realized he was on to something. He closed the exhibition, returned to his barn and over the next ten weeks finished the Mississippi sections of the painting and added views of the Ohio and Missouri Rivers. He re-opened his lectures and exhibit at the Apollo Rooms on October 19, 1846 and closed October 31. "The great three-mile painting," declared the *Morning Courier* "is destined to be one of the most celebrated paintings of the age" (Louisville *Morning Courier* 29 June 1846).

After gathering written testimonials from various local and state officials on the geographical accuracy of the Panorama, Banvard bundled up his massive painting into several large boxes and headed for Boston on the steamer *Clipper*. At Brownsville, Pennsylvania, he unloaded his equipment and proceeded by heavy wagon and railway to Boston. He rented Boston's Armory Hall, Washington Street, and opened in the middle of December, just before the Christmas season, advertising nightly performances, except Sundays, with matinees on Wednesdays and Saturdays. Admission was 50 cents for adults (Boston *Journal* 1 January 1847).

Honed by his long experience in frontier popular entertainment, the artist worked hard to perfect his theatrical techniques. Thomas Bricher, organist for Boston's Bowdoin Street Church, composed a series of waltzes for background music. Published as sheet music by Oliver Ditson at Boston in 1847, the waltzes, combined with the proceeds from descriptive pamphlets, "materially augmented" Banvard's income for the next several years (Howard 53; Robinson 25). Elizabeth Goodnow, the daughter of a Sudbury, Massachusetts, drygoods merchant and an "accomplished pianist," was engaged to play Bricher's waltzes. The dark, slender and attractive woman and the artist, after a short courtship, were married at the Harvard Street Baptist Church on May 17, 1848 (Edith Banvard, Notes MS. 4265, BFP; Genealogy Folder, BFP).

Banvard's Mississippi Panorama performance was carefully rehearsed and executed. Audiences were led into the darkened Armory Hall as Elizabeth played soft background music. Precisely at eight o'clock Banvard strode from the back of the house to the stage, the curtain rose, and "ordinary footlights" illuminated the first scene of the painting. Banvard, "seated on a platform" or standing, described the scenes as they passed by the spectators. He used a long pointer to direct audience attention to certain details. Viewers descended the Missouri, Ohio and Mississippi rivers to New Orleans and, at the next performance, ascended the rivers as the canvas was unrolled in the opposite direction. The painting was framed so the large machinery needed for turning the cylinders was hidden from the audience's view [2]

Banvard worked on his lectures until he no longer seemed "as uncultivated as the scenery he...delineated." His "racy anecdotes" and his "short, pithy remarks" revealed much "information on the manners and habits" of the people of the West. "Take the artist from the painting," a critic noted, "with his instructive lectures, interesting explanations, and amusing anecdotes, and you take away one of the principle attractions"[3] His lectures were about the geographical, social and scientific aspects of the Western river system, but Banvard's stories, unverifiable for the most part, demonstrated his showmanship. One of his tales, an attack by the notorious Murell gang, a band of riverboat pirates that terrorized the West for years, was an impossibility. The gang had been broken up prior to Banvard's voyages. In another tale, as Banvard's floating grocery store and theatre descended the Mississippi, a group of disgruntled customers, unable to attend a sold-out performance, cut the boat's shore rope and the craft floated several miles downstream before performers or patrons were aware of what had happened. The artist never mentioned the incident in his unpublished autobiography, and the story sounds suspiciously like one told by the Chapman Family, who had employed the young Banvard as a scene painter (See Chapter 1). Local townspeople, angered by the Chapman's *Floating Theatre's* 50-cent admission fee, "quietly cast the boat from its moorings, and before actors or audience were aware of the situation...the stream had carried them more than a mile before they got to shore again." Banvard also told the story of his trip to Boston when he passed off his panorama cylinder boxes as coffins containing casualties of the recent Mexican-American War (McDermott 22; Ludlow 569; Arrington 222).

The performance lasted for two or three hours, the length depending on Banvard's improvisational abilities and the reaction of his audience. The overall effect was apparently a nearly perfect illusion. At one Boston performance a St. Louis merchant saw his place of business in the picture and stopped the show by shouting, "That's my store! Halloa there, captain! Stop the boat—I want to go ashore and see my wife and family!" The merchant later remarked that the painting was so lifelike that "in a moment he seemed" to be back in St. Louis.[4] Stories such as this certainly didn't harm the volume of paying customers.

Audiences indeed found the illusion of the Mississippi Panorama startling. We, unfortunately, don't know much about Banvard's artistic abilities during this period. His limited technical skills stamp him as a theatrical artist and it is difficult to judge the Panorama, long since lost, as a work of art. Banvard was the subject of two retrospectives in Dubuque, Iowa, and Watertown, South Dakota, respectively, during 1992 and paintings done in his later years show a certain proficiency, particularly in color and perspective, probably attained with the aid of a *camera obscura*. Certainly when compared with the leaders of the Hudson River School and others, he wasn't very good. But the Mississippi Panorama itself was part of a theatrical event and because the painting was "in motion and had to be viewed from a distance, it was more like stage scenery than studio art." The life-like effects that captured the public imagination were a combination of motion, lighting effects, suggestion, and Banvard's entertaining performance. The viewer's eye, faced with the task of sorting out literally thousands of images passing by, received impressions rather than detail. "His distances and atmospheric effects," said an acquaintance, "were always his leading characteristics as a painter. His hills always seemed miles away with soft haze resting on them." Banvard's pictures, says Sara G. Bowerman, "were executed with [a] certain crude vigor, but without technical skill." His entry in the *National Cyclopedia of American Biography* remarks, "In rapidity of execution he never had an equal," hardly a testimonial to great art. Banvard himself, at least in the early years, realized his limitations. A London pamphlet stated that "He does not exhibit the painting as a work of art, but as a correct representation of the country it portrays and its remarkable accuracy and truthfulness." "This," a newspaper noted, "is exactly the point of view from which the work should be considered" (Boorstin 238, Robinson 7; Bowerman "John Banvard," *Dictionary* 1, 583; "John Banvard," *National* V, 327).

Audiences packed Boston's Armory Hall to see the panorama's "acres and miles of canvas." New Englanders' "scarcity of knowledge [about the West] gave such knowledge as there was a peculiar appeal" and Banvard, rather than being received as a "folk painter of geographic newsreels," was hailed as a contributor to the artistic, educational and scientific knowledge of the age.[5] After the Boston exhibition he stopped thinking of himself as a theatrical entertainer and scenic artist—which he was—but as a serious scientist and artist whose opinions and achievements merited attention. By emphasizing the educational nature of his painting—at specified times school groups were admitted free to the performance—Banvard promoted in Barnum-like fashion the Mississippi Panorama as family entertainment, above the supposedly low morals of the regular theatre. "Banvard's Panorama of the Mississippi, Missouri, and Ohio Rivers" ran at Armory Hall for over six months and attracted, according to Banvard's figures, 251,702 spectators. His profits, well over $100,000, made him a wealthy man.[6]

The Mississippi Panorama left its mark on New England literature. Writers found in its immense size and subject matter an expression of the undeveloped future of the nation. Henry Wadsworth Longfellow, working on his final draft for *Evangeline*, noted in his journal: "Went to see Banvard's diorama [sic] of the Mississippi. One seems to be sailing down the great stream and sees the boats and the sandbanks crested with cotton-wood, and the bayous by moonlight. Three miles of canvas, and a good deal of merit" (Longfellow, *Life* II, 67-68).

In Longfellow's novel *Kavanaugh*, Banvard's spectacle is presented as the antithesis to the idea that a great national literature must first be universal in nature. The pompous Mr. Hathaway lectures Mr. Churchill, a writer and Longfellow's spokesman:

> "I think, Mr. Churchill," said he, "that we want a national literature commensurate with our mountains and rivers,— commensurate with Niagara, with the Alleghanies, and the Great Lakes."
>
> "Oh!"
>
> "We want a national epic that shall correspond to the size of the country; that shall be to all other epics what Banvard's Panorama of the Mississippi is to all other paintings—the largest in the world!"
>
> "Ah!"

Literary historian Dorothy Ann Dondore says that the Panorama also served John Greenleaf Whittier as the source and title poem of *The Panorama and Other Poems* (1856) (Longfellow, *Kavanaugh* VIII, 425; Dondore 822).

His audience played out, Banvard left Boston for New York, rented a studio, leased a panorama hall adjoining Niblo's Garden at 598 Broadway, and opened his exhibition in time for the Christmas season, Monday, December 13, 1847. The New York newspapers hailed the massive painting as the "most superior exhibition ever produced before this public" and judged it "a monument of native talent and American genius." An anonymous "veteran Mississippi River traveller," whose writing style was suspiciously similar to Banvard's, wrote,

> As the curtain rises and the painting begins to move, the visitor has only to imagine himself on board the swiftest of steamers, passing on toward New Orleans, and he can enjoy the life-like and pleasing view of all the interesting scenery, towns, islands, boats, etc., that would meet one's eye between the upper regions of the Mississippi and the Gulf of Mexico. The illusion of the artist is so perfect that when you see a steamboat, it appears in its full size and dimensions, with the steam and vapor passing out of the smoke pipes, and the water splashing and foaming about the huge paddles on the sides of the boat, and so with other objects. Indeed, the whole painting appears more like a living reality than a work of art. [7]

The Boston and New York theatrical panorama performances established John Banvard as the most famous and wealthiest artist in America, and despite the fact that his work was a theatrical event, his "greatest influence was in the arts—the panorama movement itself." Artists, hoping to duplicate Banvard's critical and financial success, were "going to work in all directions, painting rivers, etc." John Rowson Smith, who promptly produced a "four-mile painting," Sam Stockwell, Henry Lewis and Leon Pomorédè all exhibited panoramas of the Mississippi, and John J. Egan and Samuel A. Hudson exhibited long paintings of other Western regions. Panoramas flourished in New England and artists strove to "satisfy or attempted to satisfy all demands that an exacting public could make on an expanding industry" (Arrington 219, 221).

Banvard remained the most successful. He was the first to exhibit a panorama of the Mississippi and his painting, despite claims to the contrary, was the longest in history. His performances, even with the homespun humor, were relatively sophisticated (in St. Louis a panorama of "The Burning of Moscow" featured a female magician-acrobat) and by emphasizing his work as family entertainment, he attracted a new audience into the theatre. Of the thousands of panoramas produced in the middle of the century, his was the only one to win widespread fame and bring its owner overwhelming financial success.

On September 12, 1848, Banvard traveled from New York to Cambridge, Massachusetts to call on Edward Everett (1794-1865), president of Harvard, ex-governor of Massachusetts, former U.S. Congressman, and a man unfortunately remembered today as the long-winded speaker who proceeded Lincoln before he gave his Gettysburg Address. Everett, among his many hats, had served as U. S. Minister to Great Britain from 1841 to 1845. Banvard sought his advice on whether he should exhibit in England and how he should go about it. Everett plainly told him that his only chance of establishing superiority over English rivals, as well as over John Rowson Smith, his American rival, was to win the patronage of Queen Victoria. As a private citizen and a showman, Banvard couldn't count on any official American government help. The proper approach, Everett counseled, was to approach the Queen indirectly by gaining access to those around her. Everett then boasted of how this same advice to P.T. Barnum resulted in the success of "Tom Thumb." Everett had introduced "Tom Thumb" to the Queen's personal physician at a private banquet. Word got back to the Queen and, her curiosity aroused by accounts of the midget's antics, she requested a command performance. The resulting publicity, said Everett, insured

Barnum's English success. Then Everett wrote out three separate letters of introduction to members of the London scientific community. Later that afternoon Banvard called on Abbott Lawrence (1792-1855), wealthy cotton mill owner, ex-Congressman and recent founder of Harvard's School of Science, who also gave the artist a letter of introduction (John Banvard Diary, 12 Sept. 1848, BFP). He was now ready to test the Mississippi Panorama in London, the capital of the panoramic art.

Banvard, Elizabeth and a secretary identified in Banvard's private diary only as Paul, arrived in Liverpool aboard the *Europa* on October 12, 1848. The next day they left for London by railway carriage and set up temporary lodgings at Morley's Hotel in Trafalgar Square until they "could find more suitable lodgings" (Diary, 14 October 1848). The next morning the artist paid a visit to George Catlin, the famous painter of American Indians, at his Indian Museum in Leicester Square. They, at least for the time being, got along famously. Both had contemporary reputations as "chain-lightning artists," alike in "temperament...and restless activity" (Robinson 6). Catlin had just returned from Paris, where panoramas were all the rage, and he advised Banvard to exhibit his painting there. Banvard, impressed by Catlin's thoughtfulness, didn't know that at that very moment Catlin was involved in a scheme to copy Banvard's panorama and pass it off as the original. Banvard was unimpressed, however, by Catlin's appearance. Dirty, unkempt and slovenly, the man looked nothing like the famous painter Banvard had expected. Catlin confessed that he was penniless, so the trusting Banvard loaned him 50 pounds, an act he would later regret (Diary, 14 October 1848 BFP).

Banvard moved the Mississippi Panorama into Egyptian Hall, that magnificent exhibition palace built by William Bullock, former Liverpool jeweler-silversmith and brilliant showman. For half a century it was London's leading exhibition hall; Catlin had presented his first series of Indian paintings there in 1840. Banvard gave a private performance for newspaper editors on November 25 and on December 6, once again just in time for the Christmas holiday trade, presented his first public shows. Performances were at 2:30 P.M. and 7:30 P.M. and admission was two shillings (London *Observer* 27 November 1848; Scrapbook BFP; *Illustrated London News* 9 December 1848).

Londoners, living in a city that had seen more than its share of panorama exhibitions, responded the same way as Bostonians and New

Fig. 4. Banvard's Panorama exhibition before Queen Victoria and the Royal Family, Windsor Castle, 1849. *Minnesota Historical Society.* Reprinted with permission.

Yorkers. The *London Observer* stated, "This is truly an extraordinary work. We have never seen a work...so grand in its whole character, so truthful in its delineation, or so interesting to the spectator." The *Morning Advertiser* was even more effusive when it remarked, "It is impossible to convey an adequate idea of this magnificent" work of art.

It is something more than an exhibition. It is a great work, which not only astonishes by its magnitude and grandeur, but it is highly instructive and interesting. It is, in fact, a work calculated to something more than gratify or amuse a vacant hour. (London *Observer,* 27 November 1848, Scrapbook, BFP; London, *Morning Advertising,* Scrapbook, BFP)

Banvard's "witty and entertaining" lectures delighted audiences. For many Londoners this was their first encounter with a frontier American. "Mr. Banvard," a newspaper reported, "tells many an amusing and illustrating anecdote; while it adds not a little to the entertainment, it affords also a glance at American character, and is not without interest and instruction." The *London Sun* thought Banvard's performance was delivered in "the most quaint and humorous style imaginable. His Yankee twang is delicious." A Miss Egan replaced Elizabeth as pianist, and a Madame Schweiso was commissioned to compose new music for the performances.[8]

Banvard and Elizabeth moved into permanent lodgings at 162 Regent Street and each day the artist would leave home for the American Minister's house in hopes of meeting a close acquaintance of Queen Victoria. He invited Charles Dickens to a private showing, assuming that Dickens would have some influence with the Queen. But the writer, unannounced, attended a performance with the general public instead, later sending Banvard a polite note. Undaunted as always, Banvard called on George Bancroft (1800-1891), scholar, diplomat, and America's first great historian, all through the winter. Appointed "envoy extraordinary and minister plenipotentiary" by President James Polk in 1846, Bancroft was the highest ranking American official in England.[9]

One day in January 1849, Banvard was making a pest of himself at the Bancroft home when Elizabeth Davis Bliss Bancroft, the minister's wife, introduced the artist to Amelia Murray, maid of honor to the Queen. This was the opportunity the artist had been waiting for. He invited Miss Murray and Mrs. Bancroft to a private showing of the

Panorama that very evening and the two women agreed to come. Banvard then rushed out and had one of his pamphlets, in his words, "beautifully bound in crimson velvet and gold for to get in Her Majesty's hands in some manner." The strategy worked; the Queen read the pamphlet, heard Murray's account of the exhibition, and summoned Banvard for a command performance at St. George's Hall in Windsor Castle on April 11, 1849. The Queen, Albert, young Prince Edward, and several members of the royal family attended the performance. It was a smashing success and for the rest of his life, Banvard considered this his greatest moment. He was also confident that the Queen's recognition would assure him a lifetime income (Banvard MS. 6302).

But his triumph, like so many events in Banvard's life, was short-lived. During the 1849-50 theatrical season 50 mammoth panoramas were exhibited in London and several were advertised as the original Mississippi panorama. Banvard's most serious rival, just as he had predicted, was John Rowson Smith (1813-64). Smith's business partner and manager, Professor Risley, a New Jersey-born circus acrobat who would later lead the first Western theatrical troupe into Japan, informed English audiences that Smith's first Mississippi panorama was shown in Boston in 1839, but unfortunately it was destroyed by fire. Smith, Risley solemnly intoned, worked laboriously for five years and exhibited another in 1844, two years before Banvard's Louisville debut (McDermott 50). For the first time Banvard's virtual monopoly on American panoramas was threatened. He issued a pamphlet in 1849 that warned

> The public should be on their guard against several spurious copies and incorrect imitations which have been hurriedly prepared by parties of unprincipled persons, who are now endeavoring to palm them off as being original in various parts of the country; thus robbing Mr. Banvard of the fruits of his years of toil and danger. (McDermott 47)

The hint of desperation in this advertisement was real. Banvard hastily solicited testimonials from Edward Everett ("Mr. Banvard...is the originator and inventor [sic] of this enormous class of paintings"), Charles Dickens, and Bayard Taylor (1825-1878), arguably the nineteenth-century's greatest travel writer. Banvard was further incensed when he discovered that George Catlin, fellow painter and showman, but now an embittered, broken man whose wife and youngest child had recently died, was charging Banvard with copying scenes of the Upper Missouri and Mississippi Rivers from Catlin's own paintings of the regions. Banvard counterattacked by charging that Catlin and others painted Risley and Smith's panorama *in England* by sending art students to Egyptian Hall to hurriedly sketch Banvard's scenes as they whizzed by. Banvard's charges may have been true. London audiences grew tired of Catlin's endless Indian exhibitions and he and his three daughters lived in poverty in Waterloo Street. He often took on odd painting jobs to survive. And when Englishman W.A. Brunning, aged 31 and a member of the Society of British Artists, died in 1850, Banvard gleefully noted in his diary that his *Sunday Times'* obituary had credited him with being the "principle painter on 'Risley's panorama of the Mississippi' " ("Mr. John Banvard"; Roehm 315; Diary [1850]).

Banvard was now "running scared," for instead of securing his rightful place as the preeminent London showman, the controversy only re-ignited the panorama industry, "which for years had been languishing for want of novelties" (Altick 205, 206). As panorama exhibitions sprang up all over the place, Banvard hired someone to fill in as lecturer and locked himself in his studios, producing the western bank of the Mississippi—the original painting was of the eastern bank—and new views of the Missouri and Ohio Rivers. He also added scenes from the Ohio to the original. Then, leaving his hired lecturer behind at Egyptian Hall, Banvard launched a tour of the provinces hoping to keep one step ahead of Smith and the acrobat. For the next two and one-half years the painting toured Edinburgh, Leamington, Bath, Leeds, York, Halifax, Worcester, New Port, Cheltenham, St. Leonard's Cardiff, Merthyr, Swansea, Jersey, Brighton, and Dublin, Ireland. By the winter of 1850-51, the London panorama performance had drawn 604,524 viewers, while the provincial tour had a total audience of 95,976 (*Oxford Chronicle* BFP).

Now sufficiently confident that he had beaten Smith and Risley and the other competitors, Banvard traveled to Paris, where he left Elizabeth and their two children, and disappeared for a whole year to gather sketches for a panorama of the Nile River and the Holy Land, a particularly popular subject for panorama viewers. With William A. Lilliendahl, a New York businessman, as his companion, he traveled throughout Egypt, ascended the Nile River, and made "drawings of all the antiquities and scenery along it banks." He also collected several ancient artifacts. Next he made his way through Palestine to Jordan and the Dead Sea. Back in Paris, armed with thousands of sketches, he began a Panorama of the Nile and the Holy Land, but it turned out to be a long-term project. Elizabeth had given birth to their third child during Banvard's absence, and the growing size of his family along with Elizabeth's homesickness for New England relatives, prompted Banvard to pack up both his Mississippi River panoramas, leave Paris, close down his European operations, and return to America. The Banvards arrived home in the spring of 1852 (Diary [1852]).

Banvard was moderately successful back in the States, but as the years wore on, enthusiasm for his paintings, despite his vigorous promotional efforts, wore out. In a later chapter we shall look at his theatre activities, but his panorama exhibitions were now a shadow of what they once were. Ironically, he created a mass audience for pictorial realism—well over two million people saw the Mississippi Panorama in America and Europe—and then was unable to satisfy increasing public demands for it. By the late 1860s his audience had deserted him for a medium that offered more exciting moving pictures—the melodramatic stage spectacle featuring a combination of moving panoramas, live horses on treadmills, and women dressed in flesh-colored tights, along with fog and smoke and other enticements. This development in "realism" was in turn eclipsed by the invention of the motion picture camera.

The fate of the massive Mississippi Panorama remains a mystery. Banvard took it with him to Watertown, South Dakota, the frontier settlement he called home after leaving New York in 1883. A grandson remembered playing among the cylinder rolls as a child. Local Watertown tradition says the painting was cut up and used as house insulation against the bitter South Dakota winters. Edith Banvard, the artist's youngest child and last known person to have seen the Panorama, commented in 1936 that the painting, cracked from years of travel and exhibition, was probably sold in pieces for theatre scenery.[10]

In March 1943, Edith christened a World War II Liberty ship in her father's name at Baltimore's Bethlehem-Fairfield shipyard. At the dedication ceremonies the United States Government officially recognized John Banvard as "the first motion picture producer." Three years later, after several mishaps at sea, the USS Banvard was

Part Two

Child Prodigies, Museums and European Visitors

Chapter 4
Infant Phenomena:
The Bateman Sisters on Stage

Nineteenth-century American mass audiences craved novel entertainments, such as showboats, moving panoramas and the white minstrel shows previously discussed, and they usually got it. Even relatively staid managers of legitimate theatres attempted to appease audience appetites by booking such "dramatic" wonders as Professor McCormick, "The Human Fly," who walked upside down on, or more precisely under, a 20-foot marble slab, and the incredible Mr. S.K.G. Ellis, an unfortunate individual born without arms who could "nevertheless with perfect ease to himself write, draw, cut various articles of taste with scissor, and shoot with bows and arrows" with his feet.[1] There were dwarfs like the Irish Mr. Allhead (who called himself "all head and no body") and giants like Mr. Randall, the seven-foot, six-inch "Scotch [sic] Thespis" who appeared with his giantess wife in numerous popular melodramas. The play *Mazeppa*, which made Adah Issacs Menken (1835-68) a household name as a tortured heroine in flesh-colored tights strapped to the back of a live horse, and the transvestism of Charlotte Cushman (1816-76) were all feature attractions in a never-ending parade of American theatrical curiosities. But no curiosity had the impact, serious critical consideration, or sheer wonderment of H.L. and Sidney Bateman's little girls, Kate and Ellen. From 1846 through 1854 these diminutive but talented sisters took America and England by storm, performing adult roles in Shakespeare and children's roles in light comedies. Their career epitomizes a special category in the catalogue of bizarre nineteenth-century acts—the infant phenomenon.

Child stars are an American tradition, a phenomonen that has stretched into the late twentieth century with the likes of Jackie Coogan (1914-84), Judy Garland (1922-69), Shirley Temple (1928—), Macaulay Calkin (1980—) and others. But no period surpasses the mid-1800s for the sheer number of children appearing in live theatrical events or the degree of seriousness with which they were taken. And, unlike their modern counterparts, they more often than not drew recognition by playing *adult* roles. The craze began in England where William Henry Betty (1791-1874), "Master Betty, the Young Roscius," astonished critics and audiences alike with his virtuoso acting ability. He reached his peak in 1804, at 13 years of age, when the British Parliament, in a motion introduced by William Pitt himself, adjourned to catch his Hamlet at Drury Lane. He was so sensational and gathered such a popular London following that the greatest actor and actress of the era, John Philip Kemble (1757-1823) and Sarah Siddons (1755-1831), temporarily retired from the stage rather than compete with him.

Master Betty was quickly followed by successors in America and the list of child stars seems endless—John Howard Payne (1791-1852), composer of "Home, Sweet Home;" Fanny Vining (1829-91); Clara Fisher (1811-98); the violinist Munrico Dengremont, who enlivened the notorious musical *The Black Crook* and its risqué chorus line; Mary Gannon (1829-68); and Mary McVicker (1848-1881) who later married Edwin Booth. The careers of these children were, as one might expect, short, but their performances were taken seriously. In 1836 Solomon Smith performed alongside a Miss Meadows in Mobile, Alabama, and the tall gangly actor and the tiny child were audience favorites. She played, nineteenth-century theatre manager Noah Ludlow notes without elaboration, "many children's characters, and many that were not proper to be played by children." Miss Meadows, like most of these precocious children, failed to make the transition to adult acting. When she reached the age of sixteen, Ludlow tells us, "her attraction began to weaken; her voice was not as good as it had been; she was too large for children's characters, and not quite womanly enough for leading ladies. I was told that she married early in life and left the stage" (Ludlow 452-53).

The reasons for audiences readily accepting five- or six-year-olds playing, for example, Hamlet, Shylock or, a particular favorite, Richard III, is somewhat baffling. David Grimsted, a respected critic of nineteenth-century melodrama, makes the case for the appeal of the naturalness of innocent children (although Richard III is certainly not an innocent *character*) and this quality was contrasted with what audiences perceived as the adult actor's often overwrought, declamatory, and patently artificial "art" (Grimsted 105-06). One student of the Bateman's career, Robert Badal, felt that nineteenth-century American audiences hungered for novel stage acts like the sisters' because of the lack of genuine native drama, the boredom that resulted from predictable and repetitious stock pieces, and the phenomonen of the traveling star which created the desire to always look for something new coming down the road. Children, natural objects of sentimental affection in the nineteenth century, were logical entries in the competition for the novel entertainment dollar (Badal 207-54).

Confusion exists about the actual birth dates of Kate Josephine and Ellen Douglas Batemen. Kate, fair-complexioned, delicately beautiful, was probably born in 1842; Ellen, the shorter of the two, swarthy, somewhat masculine in appearance—she always wore a pasted-on moustache as Richard III—was born in 1844. In the best American show-business tradition, the more their careers prospered, the younger became the "official" ages of this sister act that theatre historian George C.D. Odell labeled "little pests" (Odell VI, 199).

The sisters were born into a theatrical family. Their father, Hezekiah Linthicum Batemen (1812-1875)—he preferred the initials H.L. and most of his acquaintances mistakenly thought that his first name was Henry—was born in Baltimore. His early years are clouded in obscurity. In 1834, at age 22, he joined the Ludlow and Smith Company in St. Louis where, as a versatile member of the stock company, he was judged to be "pretty good." H.L. played Laertes in *Hamlet*, "attempted" Shylock for his summer season benefit, and generally played second-banana roles in farces and burlettas (Carson 268; 290-91). The truth, which took a few years for H.L. to realize, was that he was a second-rate performer. But he possessed a shrewd eye for talent and a gift, if not exactly in the league of his later partner P.T. Barnum, for promotion and publicity.

In 1839 he married Sidney Frances Cowell (1923-1881), who, even as a young girl, was as headstrong and sure of herself as H.L., and their relationship weathered many a professional and personal storm. Sidney was born in New York or New Jersey, historians are unsure which, and grew up on a farm in Ohio. Her father, born in England but a naturalized U.S. citizen, was the singing comedian-manager Joe Cowell (see Chapter I); her mother was Cowell's second wife, Frances Sheppard. Sidney moved to St. Louis in August 1839 with her family to work for Ludlow and Smith. Now 16 years of age, she fell in love with Batemen and three months after meeting they were married. The union produced four daughters, all of whom became successful actresses—Kate, Ellen, Virginia Frances (1853-1940) and Isabel Emilie (1854-1934) (Robinson *et al* 58). Sidney was a beautiful, brainy woman and many knowledgeable observers considered her the "power behind the throne" in the Bateman Family business (Moses II, 699). She was a successful playwright, an actress, certainly a successful acting coach, and in her mature years managed both the Lyceum and Sadler Well's Theatres in London, a remarkable business accomplishment for a woman in the nineteenth century.

Kate and Ellen made their stage debut in Louisville in 1846. The two children playing the roles in *The Children of the Wood* fell ill, and four-year-old Kate and Ellen, less than two years old, took their place. The sentimental melodramatic plot concerned a brother (Kate) and a sister (Ellen) under the care of a dypsomaniacal uncle, brother to their father, who thinks the children's parents are dead. He orders his two servants, one of whom, the kindly Walter, was played by H.L., to kill the children so that he can inherit his brother's estate. Walter refuses and sets the children loose. In a particularly lachrymose section of the play, and a perfect scene for frontier audiences, the children are hopelessly lost in the woods and cling to one another, bemoaning their terrible fate. The scene never failed to move an audience to tears. But fate intercedes, the parents return alive, the evil uncle is unmasked, Walter is rewarded, and everyone lives happily ever after (Badal 34).

Louisville audiences were electrified by these tiny sisters' performance and H.L. immediately realized he had a moneymaking act on his hands. Kate and Ellen were quick studies and reportedly eager to learn. H.L. and Sidney shrewdly changed their repertoire and coached the sisters in children's roles in burlettas, burlesques, and melodramas like *The Swiss Cottage, The Hunter of the Alps, Metamora, The Spoiled Child*, as well as meatier roles in Shakespeare's and Colley Cibber's notorious "improvements" of Shakespeare—*Macbeth, Hamlet, The Merchant of Venice*, and *Richard III*. The parents' hunch that infant prodigies would attract frontier audiences paid off and within a year husband and wife were playing supporting roles to their precocious children. Using *Richard III* as their primary vehicle—Kate as Richmond, Ellen as Richard—the Batemen family traveled the Ohio and Mississippi Valleys by steamboat, playing all the large theatres and earning applause and money wherever they went.

A body of anecdotes grew up around the children, but hard evidence is not always easy to come by. Kate apparently enjoyed playing cards with Mississippi riverboat gamblers; her favorite game was Old Maid. In 1851 *Lennox's Floating Theatre*, the showboat on which they were performing, caught fire. After the flames were doused, Kate calmly returned to her card game with adult professional gamblers (Badal 51-2). Stories such as this make it difficult to know the difference between the girls' true personalities and the *persona* created by their parents and, later, by P.T. Barnum. H.L. and Sidney jealously guarded the children's privacy unless a publicity stunt was necessary to hold them up to public view. A reporter for the Milwaukee *Daily Sentinel* interviewed them in 1850 and found "that in the privacy of the home they are even more natural and affectionate then children who are not thus gifted." They displayed "beautiful traits of character" (Milwaukee *Daily Sentinel*, 8 Nov. 1850), whatever that meant. Numerous surviving portraits aren't very helpful, either. Kate was indeed a beautiful child and Ellen, complete with moustache, does indeed look masculine—not boyish, but masculine—with her rounded facial features, thickset body hidden by a cloak, and short, muscular-looking arms. But their true personalities as children remain a mystery.

The Bateman parents worked long hours drilling the girls in elocution, gesture and movement, and the sisters' ability to mimic adult mannerisms, while occasionally inconsistent, was uncanny. By 1849 the parents decided they were ready for the East. They first appeared in April 1849 in Boston, where they performed the fifth act of Colley Cibber's awful reworking of *Richard III*. The young girls, despite publicity to the contrary, more often than not played *scenes* from Shakespeare rather than full-blown productions. This lessened the amount of lines they had to learn, kept the number of actors to hire at a minimum, and increased the amount of rehearsal time available to perfect the act. They went on to New York where they opened at the Broadway Theatre on December 10 with scenes from *Richard III* and *The Spoiled Child* (New York *Herald*, 10 Dec. 1849). They were the hit of the New York season, catching the eye of P.T. Barnum (1810-91), a man who was no stranger to infant phenomena. Barnum throughout his long career showed a predilection for "surrounding himself with appeals to the childlike" and he also cornered the market on child stars. Curiosities and attractions such as Charles Stratton, "Tom Thumb"

(1838-83), Clara Fisher, Jenny Lind (1820-87), and his endless beautiful baby contests were examples of the showman's ability to tap into the wellspring of infant devotion and "many of his greatest exhibits represented either the innocence of the child and the naif, or exploited the sense of lost innocence in adults" (Harris 286).

Barnum signed the whole family to an exclusive contract, which mutually benefited both parents and Barnum, but which later backfired in 1855 when Barnum, facing yet another bankruptcy, took H.L. to court to recover $4,000 the family owed him (Saxon 194). But for now everything was rosy. The girls opened in Philadelphia at Barnum's American Museum during February 1850, where they competed for audiences daily with the "Fegee Mermaid," a singing dwarf, a portrait of Jenny Lind, a "Hydrogen-Oxygen Microscope," and "700,000" other additional wonders. The Bateman Sisters were, declared the Philadelphia *Public Ledger,* the "wonders of the age" (Philadelphia *Public Ledger*, 18 Feb. 1850; qtd. Badal 66). Barnum brought the family back to New York in 1850 to work in his famous American Museum at Broadway and Ann Streets (see Chapter 5). They arrived under a deluge of the kind of publicity only Barnum could produce. Kate, now eight, and Ellen, six, according to Barnum were earning "$1000 a week!" for their heavy fare of Shakespeare and their light comedies. They left New York in the summer, hitting the rivers again—Milwaukee, Chicago, Louisville, and Jackson and Vicksburg, Mississippi.

Barnum then, as he had done successfully with the young "Tom Thumb," launched the girls on a tour of London and the provinces. They debuted at the St. James Theatre on August 23, 1851. The Bateman family arrived in London amidst strained relations between the American and British theatre communities. In 1849 several injuries and deaths occurred during an ugly riot at New York's Astor Place Opera House. This tragedy was the result of a running feud between American idol Edwin Forrest (1806-72), that bombastic actor whose rough, manly and untutored acting style symbolized the American continent itself, and William Charles Macready (1793-1873), an irascible curmudgeon who was acknowledged as England's finest actor at the time. The transatlantic bickering between these two came to represent a young American republic flexing its cultural muscle within a society still dominated by British art and culture. The Bateman Sisters, with their natural charm and precocious talents, went a long way to repair, at least for the British side, the damage done by the foolish, but ultimately deadly, feud between Forrest and Macready and their supporters.[2]

While British audiences were warm and receptive, most critics, except for the *London Illustrated News,* which called them the "pitch of perfection," reacted with disgust (*London Illustrated News* 30 Aug. 1851). The writer for *The Athenaeum* thought their work was "something painful and revolting." Ellen as Richard III so mimicked the gestures and vocal quality of Edmund Kean that she was "evidentally...drilled by some one well acquainted with the style of that great actor, and [was] elaborately wrought into a miniature resemblance of him." The children were "unwholesomely developed," the critic said, "already turned into machines" (*The Athenaeum* 16 Aug. 1851; 30 Aug. 1851). But audiences didn't care. Barnum wrangled a benefit for the sisters thrown by the Duchess of Somerset and the Turkish and Austrian ambassadors, and had them interviewed by the Prince of Wales. Although it would later backfire, Barnum felt, as did other American showmen (see Chapter 3), that attention from British royalty provided instant publicity back in an America still fascinated with titled foreigners.

In 1852, praised by royalty and commoner alike, the sisters returned to a New York backlash when they appeared at, of all theatres, the Astor Place, site of the notorious 1849 riot. Their New York publicity, smugly noted the *Herald,* (New York 22 May 1852) revealed the "unlimited puffery lavished on them by the English press," and the Batemans, much to their surprise discovered that audiences and critics had tired of their Shakespeare act. More ominously, they were found wanting in their child impersonations. Apparently Kate and Ellen were so skilled at portraying adults they were no longer believable as children! They moved to Barnum's American Museum once again, taking their place, says G.C.D. Odell, "with other freaks of nature" (Odell V, 517).

H.L. and Sidney fired Barnum, or he fired them, and faced with changing tastes, withdrew Shakespeare from their repertoire and limited the sisters' acting to children's roles in slight and inconsequential comedies such as their old war horses *The Spoiled Child* and *Bombastes Furioso.* During the next two theatrical seasons, the family toured the East and South (Washington, D.C.; Charleston, South Carolina; New Orleans), appeared in the Mississippi and Ohio River Valleys again (Louisville and Chicago), and then went back to Boston. In 1854, the

Bateman Family moved to California seeking, like so many troupers, fresh audiences in the larger cities such as San Francisco and Sacramento and boom towns such as Stockton and Placerville. Now aged 11 and nine, the sisters opened in San Francisco's Metropolitan Theatre on April 10, 1854. Shakespeare and Cibber were restored to their act and several new light comedies and melodramas, including their mother Sidney's *Young America; or the News Boy,* were offered.

To put it mildly, the Bateman Sisters beat anything Californians had ever seen. Audiences were "struck dumb with amazement" (*Alta California* 14 April 1854; qtd. Badal 66). It was the height of the gold rush, children were scarce, and many audiences were composed of sentimental homesick miners. One critic, Frederick Ewer, while recognizing that they were mere children, nevertheless hailed the sisters as the "first of a new race of artists...No ordinary child even with the close training of years could accomplish the miracles with which little Ellen has astounded us" and,

Nothing but genius, great, deep and inborn, can produce portrayals of character like [hers]...When we are surfeited and disgusted with mediocrity, then we shall look back with relief to the days when little Kate and Ellen Bateman burst upon the world with their startling impersonations of adult characters as well as childhood. (*The Pioneer*; qtd. Hewitt 167-68)

Then, at the pinnacle of their Western success, a bizarre incident occurred in San Francisco that spelled disaster and probably shortened their careers. H.L., who had learned a thing or two about promotion from Barnum, sponsored a playwriting contest open to any California citizen. Along with an impressive $1,000 prize, the lucky winner would earn a production of his or her play starring Kate and Ellen and a special guest star, the young Edwin Booth. The winning play, a melodrama titled *The Mother's Trust; or California in 1849*, was written by a woman who called herself "U.F.M.W.W." She informed the newspapers that she wished to remain anonymous and that her prize was to be donated to the San Francisco Orphan Asylum. As the city admired the unselfish generosity of this anonymous playwright/benefactor, an enterprising San Francisco *Chronicle* reporter broke the story that the mysterious author of *The Mother's Trust* was none other than Sidney Frances Cowell Bateman.

Despite an understandably hostile press, H.L. produced the play anyway. Sidney expressed complete surprise at winning the contest, and admitted, rather ungraciously considering the other 20-odd playwrights who had entered, that she had *"hastily scribbled* the simple drama the committee have selected as the best." The bitterness surrounding the incident came to a head when Frank Soule, the editor of the *Chronicle*, printed a scathing attack on Mrs. Bateman's acting ability. H.L. defended his wife's honor on the streets of San Francisco, squaring off against Soule in true gunfighter fashion. H.L. fought both Soule and a friend of his, M. Wilson, when a fourth party, another friend of Soule's named Newhal, entered the fray. Newhal drew and fired his pistol; H.L. fired back. Miraculously no one was seriously injured, although Soule received a slight gunshot wound. H.L. was arrested and jailed under $5,000 bond. He had seen the light; he paid a $300 fine and the Batemans left California, never to return. After only six months, the California tour had ended (Badal 123-25).

The family left California in disgrace, although it must be pointed out that Kate and Ellen were never blamed for their parents' blunders. Obviously shaken by the incident, H.L. decided to launch the girls on a long farewell tour and then retire. They returned to New York and Louisville and began a long engagement in St. Louis. Now teenagers they found audiences less willing to accept them as child prodigies and the girls' interest in appearing together on stage gradually dwindled. They made their last joint appearance in 1856 at the St. Louis Theatre, now managed by H.L. and Sidney. Thus ended the most successful careers of any nineteenth-century child stars.

Ellen never set foot on a stage again, choosing instead at age fifteen to marry Claude Greppo, a French silk salesman. They settled down in St. Louis, where she lived a quiet, domestic life for the next 76 years. She died at age 91 in 1936, her passing apparently unnoticed by the local newspapers who didn't print an obituary. Kate resumed her acting career, becoming an adult star as Leah the Jewess in *Leah the Forsaken*. In 1863 the play ran 211 consecutive performances at the Adelphic Theatre in London. She married English physician George Crowe and permanently settled in England (Robinson *et al* 59). Ironically, while Ellen, considered the greater talent of the two, never acted again, Kate acted professionally for the next 56 years, and at one time was managed by Augustin Daly (1838-99), one of America's greatest theatrical innovators and a man who possessed a good eye and ear for talent. In 1881 she was forced to retire from the London stage for several years because of a painful and incurable facial disease. Her last stage appearance was in a 1912 play ironically titled *The Younger Generation*. She died in 1917.

After the sisters retired, H.L. and Sidney, ever the opportunists, never missed a step. Sidney continued writing plays, including *Self*, a popular comedy of manners whose plot closely resembles Anna Cora Mowatt's more famous play *Fashion*, and both parents became competent theatre managers. After running several American theatres—the St. Louis Theatre and New York City's Wallack's Theatre, French's Theatre, and Pike's Opera House—and managing Kate for a time, H.L. and Sidney moved to London. There they leased the Lyceum Theatre and managed Kate and yet other daughters, Isabella and Virginia, to stardom. Isabel was matched with an up and coming young provincial actor named Henry Irving (1838-1905), who became the first actor to be knighted and whose accomplishments overshadowed them all. When H.L. died in 1875, Sidney took over management of the Lyceum and later ran the Sadler's Wells theatre. She died of pneumonia in January 1881. Isabel, who played Ophelia in Irving's famous production of *Hamlet*, retired from the stage in 1899 and became an Anglican nun. Virginia married the prominent actor-manager Edward Compton (1854-1918), and the couple played leading roles at the first Shakespeare festivals at Stratford-on-Avon. She died at age 87 in 1940, a respected and influential member of the English theatre community (Robinson *et al* 61).

The unusual careers of Kate and Ellen Bateman pose several interesting questions. Were they genuine actors or merely curiosities? Were they precocious children engaged in imitating their elders or were they authentic prodigies? And is there any way of knowing? They were certainly prodigies of a kind. The long memorized roles, grueling travel conditions, frequent performances all required children with exceptional determination. No record exists, aside from an occasional illness, that they ever had an "off" night. This consistency—they performed nearly every night from 1854 to 1856—is a testament to their fortitude. It may also indicate the driving ambition of their parents.

Critics were divided over the nature of the sisters' "art." They loved them in the provincial theatres, many finding them equal or superior to their adult counterparts in Shakespearean roles. The Buffalo *Morning Express* drama critic declared, "We have seen them sustain difficult characters with better judgment than often marks the efforts of mature years" (Buffalo *Morning Express,* 23 Oct. 1849). But dissenting urban critical voices about the Batemans and prodigies in general were in the majority. Theatre historian G.C.D. Odell dismissed them as "little pests." Laurence Hutton emphatically stated "in no case is the Infant Phenomonen upon the stage—thespian, terpsichorean, harmonica, gymnastic, or abnormal—to be encouraged or admired...[they do not] educate the masses; [they do not] not advance art; [they do] nothing which it is the high aim of the legitimate actor to do." *The Athenaeum* critic thought their efforts "unnatural exertions" and found it appropriate that Barnum, "the American Monster-monger," would present a theatrical act that was "impossible to treat as a matter of art" (Hutton 221, 222; *The Athenaeum* 16 Aug. 1851). If *The Athenaeum* writer was correct that Kate and Ellen had been turned into machines, then H.L. and Sidney played a much larger role in their children's "genius" than any other contemporaries were willing to admit. The nagging suspicion remains that the sisters were clever, thoroughly trained and mere children after all. As with so many infant phenomena, they were not admired for their acting, but because they were *children* acting. That they were special young women there can be no doubt. That they were great actors seems far-fetched.

Chapter 5
Banvard's Museum and Theatre, Broadway and Thirtieth Streets: A Study in Theatre Failure

In 1811, John Howard Payne (1792-1852), former child star and serious man of the theatre, went to the circus. He watched the delighted reaction of the audience to this new entertainment and decided that the "insatiable thirst for novelty which constitutes a predominant feature in our national character may make the enterprise popular and lucrative." But he and "all men of taste and sense" knew that legitimate drama wouldn't associate with "this motley mixture of amusements that can never harmonize" (Grimsted 99). He was dead wrong. The nineteenth century abounded with theatrical and paratheatrical combinations. The circus grew to a hodgepodge of entertainments and by 1850 could boast not only equestrians, jugglers, clowns and menageries, but tragedies, burlesques, comic operas, rudimentary side shows, and minstrel shows. "Dr." Gilbert R. Spalding (1812-80) and Charles J. Rogers (1817-95) managed to combine almost all popular entertainments into a single operation. They mounted a circus on a showboat, *Spalding and Rogers' Floating Palace*, that employed 100 performers and crew, seated 2,500 patrons, presented regular dramas and 12 other play genres, and was towed by *The Raymond*, a small steamer that featured a complete minstrel troupe aboard (Schick, "Early Showboat and Circus" 211-225).

But another all-encompassing institution of popular entertainment came from a source more unusual than the circus—the "natural" history museum. It was popularized on a mass scale through the remarkable efforts of Phineas Taylor Barnum (1810-1891) and today he stands head and shoulders above all other nineteenth-century showmen because of it. Museum management gave Barnum his reputation for "humbuggism," his enormous wealth, and his lasting influence on American popular culture. Actually, Charles Willson Peale (1741-1827), painter, naturalist, inventor, and showman, is credited with beginning the American

69

museum movement when his Philadelphia exhibits attracted paying customers in the 1780s. His museum featured "wax figures and a notable collection of the founder's own paintings; lectures, scientific demonstrations, and musical evenings; magic-lantern shows and a scenic spectacle with changeable effects...collections of insects, minerals, and seashells, anthropological and fossil materials, historical relics" (Saxon 92).

Forty-odd years later, Barnum took over John Scudder's American Museum in December 1841. Scudder, who had modeled his establishment on Peale's collections, had died and his estate had been unable to sell the building, which stood on a favorable location at New York's Broadway and Ann Streets. Barnum bought the place for a song. He then proceeded to present a series of entertainments and exhibitions the likes of which America had never seen. He, too, displayed curiosities similar to Peale's, with stuffed and live birds and animals, collections of insects, minerals, shells, and butterflies, wax figures, paintings, statues, Indian artifacts, mummified bodies, but he extended the "lecture" room activity to include magicians, freaks, ventriloquist's, full-blown play productions, puppet shows, panoramas, dioramas, the Bateman Sisters (see Chapter 4)—the list is endless. The four-story building was crammed full—where did he put everything?—with hundreds of thousands of artifacts and unusual people. The American Museum receipts averaged $11,000 annually in the three years prior to Barnum's ownership; for the next three it averaged $30,000 and kept on climbing. Barnum eventually abandoned the idea of a "natural" history museum and turned mass merchandiser (Saxon 89-112).[1] This aggressive pursuit of profit resulted in a curious symbiotic relationship between the professional showman, of which Barnum was the prototype, and his audience. "Humbug"—that oddly appropriate word that implied a social contract in which the customer expected to be fooled by the showman— grew out of Barnum's museum days. On the other hand, the museum appealed to the American curiosity to learn how and why natural and mechanical things worked. It emphasized "individual learning and confidence" (Harris 74). During a period in which legitimate theatre was still regarded by many as sinful, the urban museum could offer entertainment that was useful, enlightening and safe for families. Menageries were "educational;" dramas, "moral;" fine arts, "edifying;" weird freaks of nature, "scientific literacy." Barnum's notorious hoaxes were accepted within this framework, and if one hoax—and there were hundreds, if not thousands, perpetrated—was exposed, Barnum carefully orchested a "pattern of planted objections, denials, and counter charges," and the resulting publicity merely increased the museum's attendance. The practical joke "survived in a skeptical society," Neil Harris shrewdly observes,

> Because it was a way of reducing a hostile and threatening environment to human scale by manipulating its elements and so demonstrating control over them. The tall tale, the put-on, the travel lie, were social conveniences and even the most hardheaded Yankee peddler could participate in their creation or enjoyment. (Harris, *Humbug* 71-2)

In 23 years time, in a country of 35 million, Barnum sold 38 million tickets (Saxon 105).

The success of Barnum's American Museum spawned numerous imitators, most of whom, like George Wood or George B. Bunnell, Barnum either bought outright or forced into silent partnerships. Only one competitor, panoramist John Banvard in 1867 and 1868, gave Barnum a genuine run for his money with his Banvard's Museum and Theatre. In the end, Banvard, like the others, failed, but in an era dominated by the figure of P.T. Barnum, the artist's story of failure provides an interesting contrast to the familiar story of Barnum's successes.

John Banvard returned from Paris to America in 1852 as "the most famous artist in the world" and "one of the wealthiest men on earth" (Scrapbook, BFP). He continued displaying the Mississippi Panorama and introduced the Nile Panorama, 48 feet high and an eighth of a mile long, and a Holy Land Panorama. Banvard now thought he was on equal footing with P. T. Barnum, although he never stated his reasons for wanting to emulate the master showman Barnum. Perhaps he craved publicity or wanted to make a greater impact on American culture. He certainly possessed enormous reserves of capital that it would appear gave him lifetime security and he expressly wanted to settle down and take his place among the country's social and cultural elite.

But first he needed a home. Barnum had constructed his monstrous Fairfield, Connecticut, home "Iranistan," modeled after Brighton's Royal Pavilion, and made it "as fabulous a place as showman or any person ever occupied" (Saxon 157). Banvard decided he deserved nothing less, so he bought 60 acres near Cold Spring Harbor on the north shore of Long Island and spent the years between 1852 and 1855 and a good deal of his money constructing a replica of Windsor Castle, retreat of British royalty and site of his greatest triumph as a showman.

His castle, officially christened Glenada after his daughter Ada (1852-1920), was completely designed inside and out by the artist himself. Two years were spent in constructing the home; one full year alone was devoted to landscaping the grounds. It took so long to build and so much money that neighbors never referred to the home as Glenada Castle; they called it "Banvard's Folly."

The artist took full advantage of his new status and promptly retired. After 20-odd years of rootlessness, of meandering across America, Europe, Africa, and the Near East, he now had a family and a castle. He played the part of country squire to the hilt, opening the grounds of his estate, as Barnum had done, to the general public, attending church regularly, lecturing at Temperance Society meetings, and taking neighborhood children for long rides in his pony cart. In 1860, he threw a party, which he called a "Fair Extraordinary, after the manner of the English Fairs and Fetes of France." He also footed the entire bill for the expensive New Shore Road that led from Cold Spring Harbor to its steamboat landing. And he still painted. Everywhere. Just as he'd done on the frontier, he painted public murals, "largely of horses and dogs," for area businesses, including Totten's Livery Stable and the local blacksmith's shop (Newman 83, 96).

By the 1860s, however, Banvard's income was sharply reduced when audiences deserted panorama halls for melodramatic stage spectacles that used the moving panorama for heightened realistic effect. Out of the public limelight for 12 years, Banvard decided to stage a comeback, only this time, instead of anticipating public taste, he jumped into the middle of a movement that was already underway. Others had gotten there before him, and this time he couldn't adjust. He devoted himself full time to designing and painting large-scale theatre panoramas, playwriting, and theatre management. The first result of his literary and scenic efforts, a "biblical-historical" drama entitled *Amasis, Or, The Last of the Pharaohs,* opened at the Boston Theatre on September 19, 1864 and ran for six performances. Banvard spent months painting the scenery for this massive production, and it's likely that he copied or used portions of his Nile Panorama. The leading roles in the play, Amasis and Apries, were taken by two respectable Boston and New York actors, Edward Loomis Davenport (1815-77) and James W. Wallack, Jr. (1818-73), respectively. The size of the opening night audience was boosted by a contingent of the International Order of Odd Fellows, who were holding their national convention in Boston. They witnessed, said the *Boston Journal*, "fine scenery, elegant costumes, and a highly interesting play based upon a new subject with vigorous language and exciting situations." The plot was "well worked up." The critic for the *Boston Morning Advertiser,* however, found the production "somewhat tame," and, in a defect that consistently plagued American theatre in the 1800s, Edwin L. Davenport "was hampered by an imperfect knowledge of his part." "The play," the *Morning Advertiser* critic continued, "will be repeated and many little accidents and faults, which are not easily to be helped at a first performance will doubtless be avoided...The scenery is very good indeed, the last scene being extremely well managed and effective" (*Boston Journal* 20 Sept. 1864; *Boston Morning Advertiser* 20 Sept. 1864).

Amasis, with its "well worked up" plot, would be the first and last Banvard theatrical venture to receive *any* kind of favorable critical notice. But his success with *Amasis* inspired him to launch a full-time career as a theatrical entrepreneur. These must have been heady days; he had progressed from a penniless itinerant entertainer bailing out leaky showboats to a fabulously wealthy showman who could afford to indulge his theatrical tastes. In 1866, he looked up his Old Nile River expedition partner William Lilliendahl at Liliendahl's business offices at 64 John Street, New York City. The artist had a proposition to make. P.T. Barnum dominated the museum entertainment industry, but a well-financed, artistically superior operation had the potential of successfully competing with the American Museum. Lilliendahl and Banvard had brought back thousands of artifacts from the Middle East, more than enough to stock a museum, and *Amasis* had shown that Banvard could control all aspects of a theatre operation. Lilliendahl, who in a later legal deposition said that he always "possessed friendly feelings" toward Banvard, was persuaded immediately. He invested $3,000 on the spot. Banvard then formed the New York Museum Association and issued a total of $300,000 worth of stock in lots of $2,000 each to several prominent New York business families, including the Beaches and the

Fowlers. Unfortunately, the artist failed to register either the Association or the stock with the State of New York. He then leased six three-story buildings at Broadway and Thirtieth Streets from Henry Schiefflin for $7,000 per year. He rented out five of the buildings, used the sixth as a museum storage area for what a bitter Lilliendahl later described as "broken and dilapidated curiosities," and built a new theatre on a large vacant lot behind the buildings.

The artist paid for the construction of the theatre by trading Association stock for materials and labor. At least two films, the Donat Lumber Company and Jones's Brick Company, furnished materials at a "very low price" in return for shares on which they paid from 60 to 80 per cent of the face value (Lilliendahl MS). Other firms supplying Banvard were Wheeler and Wilson, sewing machines for canvas; Woodward Manufacturing Company, gas fittings; Doremus and Nixon, upholstery; John Latimer, carpeting; F. King, plumbing; and R. Galbraith, taxidermy (*New York Times* 17 June 1867). Banvard had total control of all the financial arrangements for the theatre, "managing as he saw fit." He then formed a board of directors consisting of his two young sons, Eugene, age 13, and John Jr., age eight; his father-in-law, E.K. Goodnow; his nephew, W.K. Banvard; Joseph Ayres; W.R. Brown; Lilliendahl; and himself as president. Each board member purportedly bought at least $2,000 worth of shares, but Lilliendahl later testified that they, in fact, did not and he never saw a stock certificate. No board meetings were ever held (Lilliendahl MS 3307).

Despite its shady beginnings, the theatre was recognized as the finest in New York when completed. Covering 40,000 square feet, it contained rooms for lectures and museum curiosities and a three-tiered auditorium that seated two thousand (Brown II, 522). A 50-foot-long entrance to the building "terminated in a steep stairway to some nineteen steps" that led to the auditorium (Daly 314). The lecture room was built for "intellectual entertainment, particularly designed for family recreation." The museum section, billed as the first building "erected expressly for museum purposes" in New York, opened before it was ready. "The public are especially informed," Banvard apologized, "that the Museum curiosities are not arranged in the perfect manner they will be hereafter" (*New York Times* 17 June 1867). The city welcomed Banvard's open challenge to Barnum's American Museum and the *New-York Times* noted,

The New-York Museum is the name by which the long threatened rival to Mr. Barnum's moral institution shall henceforth be known, and its locality, on Broadway, within a few inches of Thirtieth-street, makes it peculiarly convenient to that portion of our population which, according to popular managerial fiction, has been heretofore isolated from the elevating influences of the drama. (*New York Times* 23 June 1867)

Banvard then assembled a "large if not brilliant" company managed by Saunders B. Duffield (d. 1879) and opened the theatre as Banvard's Museum on June 17, 1867 (Odell VII, 216). The museum section opened before noon and two dramatic performances were given in the auditorium daily. At the opening, the Mississippi Panorama, now probably a little worse for wear after 21 years of continuous use, was displayed in the auditorium. After the two-hour lecture-performance, Harry B. Phillips's (b.1819) recited a patriotic address written by Jonas B. Phillips. An operatic chorus sang "The Hymm of Four Nations," and the company closed with two burlettas, *Jenny Lind at Last* and *A Husband for an Hour.* It was a long evening (*New York Times* 17 June 1867). The historical drama *Rob Roy, or, Auld Lang Syne* and Professor Longrenia, a magician, were added to the bill during June and July, and a comedy, *Diavola; Nobody's Daughter, Or, The Ballad Singer of Wapping*, starring Kate Reignolds (d. 1911), ran August 12 through August 31. Admission ranged from a steep $10 for private boxes to 20 cents for children under ten years of age. General admission was 30 cents.

P.T. Barnum, although in semi-retirement at the time, met the challenge of his new uptown rival. One of the unique features of Banvard's Museum were windows and ventilation louvers ("600 square feet") that surrounded the auditorium on all sides, rendering it, in Banvard's understated publicity, "the most ventilated house, not only in America, but in the world" (*New York Times* 17 June 1867). Barnum, whose own place *didn't* have wraparound ventilation, declared, in considerably less detail but more hyperbole, that his museum contained "THOROUGHLY VENTILATED. Cool! Delightful!! Cool!!! Elegant, Spacious and Airy Halls" (*New York Times* 24 June 1867). The gauntlet had been flung. When Banvard displayed his Mississippi Panorama, Barnum exhibited a Nile panorama, a subject for which Banvard was famous and which may have been copied from Banvard's own painting. Both showmen—although by this time Banvard only referred to himself as an "artist"— displayed their own version of the Cardiff Giant, the notorious prehistoric man hoax "found" in upstate New York (Daly 314). Banvard had the original; Barnum the copy. Barnum received the most publicity.

Banvard closed the theatre on September 1, probably for financial reasons. He, of course, had paid many of the construction companies and most of the stage hands in worthless museum stock and they were demanding cash. Joseph Ayres, nominally the financial director of the theatre, spent his time "puttering around" the theatre and left every decision, no matter how trivial, to Banvard himself. The gullible Lilliendahl once again entered the picture and cosigned one promissory note for $5,000 to help Banvard out, but it was of little use (Lilliendahl MS 3307).

The struggling theatre's fortunes temporarily revived in October when producer John De Pol was engaged to stage Arthur Cuyas Armengol's ballet spectacular *The Devil's Auction, or, The Golden Branch*. De Pol allegedly hired several "excellent dancers" from Europe (Odell VII, 216; *New York Times* 27 Sept. 1867) to appear in the play. Despite exotic names like Guiseppina Morlachi, Aurelia Ricci, Catrina Corradine, Giovanni Lupo, and Domenico Ronzani, many were, in fact, American. The huge production, with dancers, singers, actors, and musicians filling the stage amidst massive scenery, was difficult to mount. Even though its stage was already five feet wider than any other in New York, De Pol convinced Banvard to widen it yet another 20 feet to accommodate the action. This meant extra rehearsals after the stage was renovated and the re-opening of the theatre was twice delayed, further draining the showman's financial resources (*New York Times* 23 June 1867; *New York Daily Tribune* 2 Oct. 1867).

Renamed Banvard's Grand Opera House and Museum, the theatre opened *The Devil's Auction* on Wednesday, October 3, 1867. "Obviously intended to rival the glories of *The Black Crook*," (Odell VII, 318) the play featured a "very slight thread of drama" and a stage full of women in tights (*New York Daily Tribune* 4 Oct. 1867). The threadbare plot concerned a peasant girl given by her miserly father to a lecherous old count, but, the *Daily Tribune* noted, "Few persons expect a ballet to contain positive merits of a literary character. It is enough if pretexts are

found for the frequent introduction of the dancers" (*New York Daily Tribune* 2 Oct. 1867). The *Times* commented, "For the drama and the way it may happen to be played, and the plot or moral or meaning of it, nobody seems particularly to care. The point of interest is, first, the dancing; next the dancers; and last, the scenery" (*New York Times* 4 Oct. 1867). Nevertheless, the four-act spectacular was "a sensation," and the titillating production sold out for several weeks. Most of the spectators were male (*New York Daily Tribune* 4 Oct. 1867).

The Devil's Auction was an unusual production for the Temperance Society speaker and churchgoing Banvard. For years P.T. Barnum refused to even call his museum performance space a "theatre," referring to it instead as a "lecture room," even though it held 2,500 people, to withstand moral objections to theatrical activity. Back in 1853, Banvard, stung by President Franklin Pierce's refusal to attend a showing of his Holy Land Panorama, confided to his diary, "The President preferred to look at Ballet girls' legs...and listen to the strains of foreign artists of doubtful reputation. How different my reception by Queen Victoria!" (Diary July 1853). Now, 14 years later, he was presenting the very fare he had once privately so deplored.

On December 3, 1867, De Pol abruptly withdrew his company and joined the Academy of Music, leaving Banvard's Grand Opera House and Museum "cold and dark at the beginning of the holiday season" (Odell VII, 319). Banvard kept the theatre closed until December 21, when, with Charles Dickens in town for a series of lecture performances, he presented an adaptation of Dicken's novel *Our Mutual Friend*. That was followed by several spectacles until March 2 when *The Octoroon*, followed by Mrs. George C. Howard in *Uncle Tom's Cabin*, took the stage. But Banvard was losing money, and theatre historian G.C. Odell notes, "One predicts failure for an enterprise falling back on such hackneyed material" (Lilliendahl MS 3307; Odell VIII, 319). The theatre closed again April 4.

The gradual fall off in income from his panorama exhibitions, the enormous expenses associated with building and maintaining Glenada Castle, and his generosity in paying for public roads and giving his family jobs left Banvard near bankruptcy. Pressed hard by creditors, Banvard frantically searched around for a buyer for the museum and theatre. Lilliendahl, probably in an act calculated to recoup some of his losses, introduced Banvard to George Wood (d. 1886) and Samuel

Colville (1825-86) and they agreed to rent the place. After extensive alterations, the theatre opened as Wood's Museum and Metropolitan Theatre on August 31, 1868 (Lilliendahl MS 3307). With Banvard safely out of the way, P.T. Barnum leased the museum rooms and, in his usual exaggeration, announced that Wood would stock his museum by "drawing largely upon the Governmental Museums and public institutions of the Old World" and "purchasing private collections of Natural History, Science, and Art." Barnum actually wound up exhibiting the Siamese Twins, Sophia Ganz the Dwarf, and a midget, General Grant, Jr., all acts that had appeared at his downtown American Museum. Barnum received a modest three percent of the gross receipts (New York Times 6 April 1868). Banvard reportedly received and kept $12,000 per year for each of the next five years in rent from Barnum, Wood, and Colville. He never paid the New York Museum Association stockholders a cent in dividends (Brown, A History of the New York Stage II, 523; Saxon 109).

It took until 1873, in the midst of the worst financial crisis in American history, for the New York Museum Association stockholders to realize they had no legal charter. Banvard had, in effect, sub-leased the theatre to Wood, Colville, and Barnum. Henry Schieffin was still the legal owner of the buildings and the theatre and all the property reverted back to him. Banvard's reputation in the New York financial community was ruined (Lilliendahl MS 3307). The artist evidently had some of his fortune left. He continued to live at Glenada Castle, although census records indicate he employed only a single servant to work the 60-acre estate (Huntington, New York). He continued his literary efforts, writing two plays entitled Sun and Ice and The Mystery of San Marco, neither of which was ever produced.[2] In 1875, he published a 672-page book called The Private Life of a King, Embodying the suppressed memoirs of the Prince of Wales afterwards George IV, of England, by John Banvard, Artist, supposedly based on the suppressed memoirs of George IV. The work was dedicated (New York: The Literary and Art Publishing Co. 1875),

To those of my
SOUTHERN FELLOW CITIZENS
among whom I spent several pleasant years of my early
life who once expressed a wish to be governed by a

BRITISH PRINCE,
in preference to submitting to the generous rule of
our Federal Union.

Unfortunately, little of the work was Barvard's; he had plagiarized whole sections of Robert Huish's *The Memoirs of George the Fourth*, published in London in 1831.

In 1876 Barvard somehow regained control of his theatre. No financial records have been discovered, but perhaps he worked out an arrangement with Schiefflin to lease the theatre and pay off his debts. The theatre re-opened for the fourth time as the New Broadway Theatre on December 26, 1876 with *Corrinia, A Tale of Sicily*, written by Barvard. The play—"clearly an adaptation of a commonplace French melodrama—was uninteresting and the performance bad." The cast, "of unequalled distinction," according to Barvard, prompted theatre historian G.C. Odell to inquire, after listing the actors, "Of how many of these has the reader ever heard?"[3] The production starred John B. Studley (1831-1910), a respectable frontier actor, E.F. Knowles, and May Hart. The theatre was "spacious and commodious," judged the *Times*, "and to render it popular the management need only see to it that an attractive entertainment is offered its frequenters" (*New York Times* 24 Dec. 1876).

But the newspaper's advice went unheeded. After eight performances of *Corrinia*, Barvard staged a combination of mediocre plays and past hits such as *Rip Van Winkle, La Jolie Bouquetiere*, and *Uncle Tom's Cabin*. On February 19, 1877, however, Barvard brought in Augustin Daly and his company and thereafter rented the stage to "companies that came in at their own risk." Barvard's reputation suffered yet another blow when playwright Harry Watkins pointed out that the February 26 production of *Inshavogue, or The Days of '98*, starring John T. Hinds, was plagiarized from his own play about the Irish outlaw Inshavogue called *Trodden Down*. The play was hastily withdrawn, and Barvard, perhaps to head off legal action, allowed Watkins, a veteran frontier actor, to present and star in his own play instead (Odell X, 218-19).

Things got worse. Clara C. Hackett (1834-1909) played *Medea* in March. On opening night her co-star, Matilda Medina, playing Creusa, fainted dead away on stage and someone had to read her part from a

script. Fanny Denham (see Chapter 7) was also in the cast. Banvard advertised Hackett as "the greatest success ever known on the New York stage," but her career was decidedly mediocre. On April 30, 1877, James Duff, Augustin Daly's brother-in-law, leased the theatre and, after a shaky start, the place "emerged as a first class house" under his management. Duff opened with F.L. Graves's *The Wonder Child, or The Follies of Earth, Air and Sea*, starring Stella Boniface (d. 1883). The season closed in early July with a production of *Mazeppa* starring Fannie Louise Buckingham (Odell X, 219). One wonders if the theatre was offering anything better than Banvard himself could come up with.

Meanwhile, all through the season Banvard searched for a buyer, and poor William Lilliendahl agreed to assist him. In February 1878, Lilliendahl asked P.T. Barnum if he was interested in purchasing the faltering enterprise. The showman tersely replied, "No sir!! I would not take the Broadway Theatre as a *gift* if I had to run it. I have but one theatre and that is all I will have" (Letter P.T. Barnum to William A. Lilliendahl 28 Feb. 1878, BFP).

In April 1878, Lilliendahl himself assumed management for a brief period. Then George Edgar (d. 1899) and Chandos Fulton leased the theatre for the 1878-79 season, opening with respected English actress Ada Cavendish (1847-95) in Wilkie Collins's *The New Magdalene*. Edgar was an amateur actor and he followed the common nineteenth practice of wealthy men and women leasing a theatre—or "buying" a single night with a stock company—in order to play leading roles. He first cast himself as King Lear and Othello and failed miserably as both. He had only "the slightest stage experience," and he was "just about as good as that fact would indicate." Marie Gordon (d. 1891) played Cordelia and Desdemona; Joseph Wheelock (1839-1908) played Edgar and Iago (Odell X, 604). On June 14, 1878, Edgar and Fulton withdrew, and the Broadway Theatre, "full of vicissitude and woe," was vacant once more (Odell X, 219).

In the autumn of 1879, Banvard finally found a new owner for his now "antiquated and dilapidated" theatre—Augustin Daly (Daly 314). Daly (1838-1899), the son of a sea captain and a soldier's daughter, was recognized as the most respected director and producer of the latter part of the century. His seriousness about drama, his production taste and wit, and his notions of adequate rehearsal time and ensemble acting set the professional standards for the legitimate theatre in America. He had just

returned from abroad where he spent a disappointing 1878-79 season trying to produce plays in England. He now looked for a permanent home in which to institute reforms in stage management. With his father-in-law's financial backing, Daly purchased the Broadway Theatre and thoroughly renovated the place (Daly 256). Daly's Theatre, 1221 Broadway, opened September 17, 1879, and "America's foremost theatre for the next two decades" had come into being. Audiences "deemed the transformation of the old Broadway Theatre a miracle of ingenuity and taste" (Felheim 23; Odell XI, 15).

John Banvard, who unwittingly turned his building over to the man who would make it a legend in the American theatre, found himself bankrupt and hounded by creditors. His efforts at theatrical management were mediocre at best and, in an era when theatre operations closed with regularity, it's surprising that he was able to hold on to the museum for as long as 12 years. During his early career as a panoramist his financial operation was a one-man enterprise. In the years between 1847 and 1865, with only the help of a single secretary, Paul—whom he later fired for stealing a few dollars from the panorama till—he earned possibly millions (Diary, July 1853, BFP). He never had a business partner, a lawyer, or an accountant. In 1867, faced with fiscal responsibility toward others for the first time, he failed to perform the most rudimentary tasks: setting up a corporation, getting stock licensed, and following conventional business practices. He persuaded prominent businessmen like the Beaches, the Fowlers, and Lilliendahl, all of whom should have known better, to invest in his theatre and museum, and as late as 1878 Lilliendahl was still willing to help him. While Banvard may not have set out to swindle his investors, his financial management certainly smacks of fraud and—something his rival P.T. Barnum would have appreciated—humbug.

Other events played a role in the failure of Banvard's Museum and Theatre. The 1873 stock market panic ruined theatres all across the country. Even Edwin Booth, the most prominent actor-manager in America, failed to hold on to Booth's Theatre. The panic created a theatrical depression that lasted for several years (see Chapter 6). Then, on December 5, 1876, two weeks before the opening of *Corrinia*, Banvard's last serious attempt to re-establish himself in the theatre business, over 300 people died in a fire during a performance of *The Two Orphans* at the Brooklyn Theatre. This catastrophe extended the theatrical depression; some New York houses suffered a 50 percent drop in attendance (*New York Times* 6-8 Dec. 1876).

Finally, Banvard failed because he could not provide the uptown audience with entertainment not found elsewhere. He set out to challenge P.T. Barnum, the acknowledged king of the showman's trade, but Barnum, despite several disastrous fires and other serious setbacks, including bankruptcy in 1855, had the reputation, the knack for publicity and the resiliency to bounce back that Banvard evidently lacked. And in a spending war, Banvard had to lose. Despite the lucrative nature of the museum business—which Banvard eventually abandoned—New Yorkers apparently preferred Barnum's offerings to Banvard's.

He sold his beloved Glenada Castle and in July 1883 moved to the remote frontier community of Watertown, South Dakota to live with his two married sons, Eugene and John Jr. He spent the rest of his life dabbling in painting and poetry and delivering chalk-board lectures about his adventures to fellow South Dakotans. In 1886, at the age of 71, he began a massive diorama of Sherman's Civil War destruction of Columbia, South Carolina. His health failing from a bad heart, his eyesight nearly gone, he completed the work and, just as he had done at the beginning of his career, toured the surrounding area with the painting. He died in Watertown in obscurity on May 16, 1891.

Chapter 6
Revolt in Milwaukee:
The 1891-1892 Pseudo "Meininger"
American Tour

During the late nineteenth century, American theatres played host to dozens of prominent European actors, most of whom played grand and tragic roles in Sophocles, Shakespeare, Corneille, Schiller and others. These actors, accompanied it seems by equal numbers of entourage members and publicity agents, basked in their fame, not to mention sizable paychecks, and their performances were lovingly recorded and remembered for years after. Francesca "Fanny" Januaschek (1830-1904), the stoutly-built, formidable-looking Czech actress, employed a lachrymatory style that enthralled audiences for years despite the fact that, until late in her career, she never spoke a word of English on stage. The Italian tragedian Tommaso Salvini (1829-1916) was this country's favorite Othello (there were no native-born candidates) as a result of five American tours between 1873 and 1889. Even Edwin Booth appeared as his Iago. And of course, there was those glittering lights Sarah Bernhardt (1845-1923) and Eleanora Duse (1858-1924), whose final American tour ended with her death in Pittsburgh. It is not generally known, however, even among theatre historians, that America also played host to a troupe of foreign actors who claimed to represent the most influential movement in modern European theatre history—the famous Saxe-Meiningen Court Theatre.

The impact of the Saxe-Meiningen Court Theatre, popularly called The Meininger, on late nineteenth century European theatrical practice now has been thoroughly documented. Duke Georg II (1826-1914), ruler of the once obscure little German duchy of Saxe-Meiningen (population 8,000), produced Shakespeare, Schiller and Grillparzer in his own personal theatre and created an effective aesthetic unity among script, actor and setting. The carefully crafted Meininger production method, demonstrated in 2,591 performances in 38 cities in nine countries, but not the United States, during extended tours between 1874 and 1890, produced "nothing less than a school of theatre for an entire continent," and the "standards [his theatre] established are still those" of professional productions today.[1] The Duke, his trusted assistant and manager (*Intendant*), the singing comedian Ludwig Chronegk (1837-1891), and his third wife, actress Ellen Franz (1839-1923), formed a triumvirate that exercised an iron hand over all aspects of the production process and achieved lasting theatrical fame for their efforts at ensemble acting (all actors alternated between large and small roles), historical accuracy in sets and costume and often frighteningly realistic crowd scenes. It was authoritarian art at its best.

From November 17, 1891 through April 11, 1892, Americans had the opportunity to witness Meininger-inspired productions when a German theatrical troupe billing itself "The Meininger" appeared in 167 performances of four plays in nine American cities. This pseudo "Meininger" tour is not without controversy. In 1981, Meininger scholar Steven DeHart flatly dismissed the tour and stated that his "survey of newspapers of those cities [on the tour] failed to discover any mention of the performances." But Roger Meersman wrote about the tour in a 1966 *Speech Monographs* article that relied heavily on American newspaper coverage of the performances (DeHart 51; Meersman 40-9). Both scholars missed out on a good theatre story, for the 1891-1892 pseudo "Meininger" tour was a comedy of errors from start to finish, and it must surely rank among the most bumbling and ineptly managed enterprises of the nineteenth-century American theatre. It began in controversy, earning good critical reviews and suffering from poor houses in New York City, and quickly degenerated in the Midwest, winding up in a backstage brawl and a date for its company in a Milwaukee municipal courtroom. The tour smacks more of the Marx Brothers than the legendary Meininger.

Negotiations for a Meininger tour of America began as early as the summer of 1886. But Ludwig Chronegk, the famous *Intendant* of the Saxe-Meiningen Court Theatre, as luck would have it, suffered a severe stroke the day before he was scheduled to embark for America to begin serious discussions about a tour. Georg II, "while anxious to demonstrate his theatre's skills in America," thoroughly distrusted American theatrical agents, and he relied heavily upon Chronegk, a shrewd manager and experienced theatre artist who was largely responsible for the Meininger's continental success, to carry out both his artistic vision and the rigid discipline necessary for managing the productions (DeHart 45, 46). Negotiations were immediately halted. Then, in July 1890, Chronegk fell seriously ill in Odessa, Russia, as result of complications from his earlier stroke, and at the conclusion of that year's tour he handed in his resignation to the Duke. Georg II halted further tours rather than continue without his right-hand man. The Meininger never left the duchy of Saxe-Meiningen again (Koller 110).

But eight months later in February 1891, Carl Rosenfeld, an ambitious New York theatrical agent, began negotiations with the Duke to re-form the Meininger and bring it to America. According to the New York *Herald*, Rosenfeld and his brothers Hugo and Theodor bought a controlling interest in the Meininger for $135,000, a transaction that seems highly unlikely. At any rate, the three Rosenfeld brothers leased the Bowery Theatre, re-named it The Thalia, and announced the impending arrival of the Meininger. It was reported that Chronegk, who was by now on his deathbed, had suggested Carl Hachmann of the Berlin Free Theatre as a possible *Intendant* for the proposed tour (New York *Herald* 24 Sept. 1891). The Rosenfeld announcement caused a flurry of controversy during that summer of 1891. Crusty Gustav Amberg, owner of New York's only other German language theatre, The Amberg, bitterly denounced the Rosenfeld claims that they had contracted the famous Meininger. In September he declared that the Saxe-Meiningen Court Theatre had dissolved for the season and

One set of its scenery went to the Court Theatre in Berlin, another set to the Munich Theatre and another set to the German Theatre in Berlin. While the company was in Russia a great portion of its properties were destroyed through some accident at the railway station. Of course, the Rosenfelds might have a few members of the company, but not enough to allow them to call it the Meininger *ensemble*. (New York *Herald* 25 Sept. 1891)

The Rosenfelds responded on September 27 by publishing a telegram, allegedly sent by the Meininger's current *Intendant*, which stated: "Complete Meininger outfit purchased by the Rosenfeld Brothers. The members of the Meininger Court Theatre engaged by the Rosenfeld Brothers. Further negotiations going on." Theodor Rosenfeld said that although Chronegk had died since the negotiations began in

February, his brother Carl had "secured the services of one of his [Chronegk's] most trusted assistants—his name escapes me at the moment—who will come to America with the troupe" (New York *Herald* 27 Sept. 1891). The inability to find an *Intendant* who could successfully manage the troupe would plague the Rosenfelds until the very end.

Veteran Meininger actor Josef Kainz (1958-1910) arrived in New York in late September for an engagement at The Amberg. Kainz rallied to his new employer's defense, dismissing as humbug the notion that the Meininger were coming to America. The company actors had "scattered to the wind," he told assembled reporters. "Habelmann is in Frankfort, Otto is in Hamburg, Bartel is in Berlin, and Frl. Lorenz is insane" (New York *Herald* 27 Sept. 1891).

Whatever the truth of the charges, countercharges, and Frl. Lorenz's mental condition, a 120-member troupe calling itself "The Meininger" arrived in New York on November 8, 1891. According to the *New-York Times*, the company included 32 speaking actors from the Court Theatre, all the supernumeraries, most of the stagehands, the chief machinist, and the property master. (Actually, only three of the actors—Mathieu Pfeil, Anna Haverland, and Hilmar Knorr—definitely can be traced to the original company, placing in doubt the accuracy of the other numbers.) Two hundred supernumeraries were to be hired in each city on the tour to supplement the famed Meininger crowd scenes. The Rosenfelds engaged Hermann Stralitz as *Intendant* (*New York Times* 13 Nov. 1891).

The *New-York Times* in its November 13 issue praised the lavish decoration accompanying the troupe. Breathlessly, the paper reported that two seven-foot candelabra, said to be the personal property of the Duke himself, were valued at $3,000, and H. Schaper's statue of Pompey stood 18 feet high. The weapons and costumes, which were said to include 600 wolf, tiger, bear and leopard skins, were valued in excess of $200,000, undoubtedly an exaggerated figure. But the exotic nature and allure of these stage properties are understandable "in an age whose characteristic sense [in the theatre was] that of the eye rather than the ear" (Osbourne 60), and when all the performances were in the German language.

The "Meininger" opened at The Thalia on November 17, 1891 with Shakespeare's *Julius Caesar*. The production struck a responsive chord with the critics and must be considered a substantial achievement. After only nine days in America, 120 Germans, most of whom probably spoke no English, opened a massive production bolstered by 200 American actors, most of whom probably spoke no German. The confusion during the rehearsal process—whose rigid discipline was a Saxe-Meiningen Court Theatre trademark—is easy to imagine. After 24 performances of *Julius Caesar,* the "Meininger" mounted Heinrich von Kleist's *The Battle* (*Die Hermannsschlacht,* 1811), a massive spectacle dramatizing the 9 A.D. revolt of German tribes against invading Roman legions. The New York *Sun* discovered that "when the scene unfolds in the streets of Teutonberg we have rude timber houses unevenly arranged close together," and this asymmetrical set was enhanced by costumes that featured brass and gold ornamented helmets decorated with eagle wings and bison horns. "Rarely, indeed," the paper marveled, "has there been seen upon any stage such a vast conception so admirably carved out" (New York *Sun* 8 Dec. 1891).

The acting in both plays was considered poor and of considerably less interest than the scenery. Since the performances were in German and unintelligible to many critics, comparisons naturally were made between German and American acting styles. The "Meininger" were guilty of displaying some of the "crustiest traditions of the Teutonic stage," grumbled the *New-York Times,* the acting too old fashioned, too like the outdated "declamations of Edwin Forrest" (*New York Times* 8 Dec. 1891). The *Sun* thought Anna Haverland (1851-1908), the troupe's leading actress, was "neither beautiful in face or form, nor is she any longer a young woman. Of rather large and matronly build, her features are too petite to be capable of deep expression, and her eyes are neither large nor expressive" (New York *Sun* 8 Dec. 1891). The individual actors were not as "natural and effective as the thunder and lightening." Only Hilmar Knorr (1847-1919), who doubled as stage manager, was singled out for praise. "A good elocutionist," he was a "man of grave demeanor and striking presence" (*New York Times* 18 Nov. 1891).

The huge mob scenes in *Julius Caesar* and *The Battle* impressed American critics. "The mob is the star," declared the *Times,* "and the crowd scenes [are] superior to anything ever seen in this country" (*New York Times* 18 Nov. 1891). But despite the perennial drawing power of Shakespeare and the novelty of Germanic tribes in *The Battle,* audiences were small. The troupe moved to the Academy of Music on December 21, and to the Harlem Opera House on December 28. Their performances were "more praised by the critics than patronized by the public" (Odell XV, 50).

The "Meininger" began their whirlwind cross-country tour at the Walnut Street Theatre in Philadelphia on January 4, 1892. The company then played in Baltimore, Washington, D.C., Pittsburgh, Cincinnati, St. Louis, Chicago, and finally, disastrously, Milwaukee. Critics in these cities echoed their New York colleagues by emphasizing three aspects of the authentic Meininger method:

(1) the democratic, but declamatory and uneven, method of acting;
(2) the meticulously detailed (at least, at the beginning of the tour) costumes and settings; and,
(3) the striking crowd scenes. This February 8, 1892, St. Louis *Post-Dispatch* review of *Julius Caesar* was typical:

In this company there are not stars, but every member is presumed to be an artist, and may be cast in any part without regard to its prominence...Finer impersonations of the principal figures in the play may be found on our stage. One misses to some extent the charms of individual greatness in the Meininger performance, but one gains on the other hand satisfaction of complete interpretation of every part of the play wrought in detail with conscientious care and artistic intelligence...

The stage settings are accurate and fine and each scene is a complete and artistic picture. The mob scene is a revelation and it presents as, it is safe to say, the playgoers of the city have never seen it presented, the Roman populace swayed by the contending eloquence of Brutus and Anthony [*sic*]. The Orators are merely parts of the scene, and the cunning oratory of Anthony [*sic*] by which, feeling his way into the sympathies of the hearers, he adroitly masters them and leads them gradually to the point of riotous madness, was never so clearly elaborated. Not a detail is neglected for the life-like representation of the scene. The mob is as important as the orator. It is a characteristic mob and its changing moods are played upon by the speaker and his henchmen and are vividly portrayed. (St. Louis *Post-Dispatch* 8 Feb. 1892)

An incident occurred in Cincinnati which changed the whole complexion of the tour. Herman Stralitz, failing the Rosenfeld's expectations as *Intendant*, was replaced by Max Schiller. Poor Max Schiller. If anyone was unprepared to handle a large company of volatile and non-English speaking actors touring a strange country, it was Schiller. A strikingly handsome, somewhat diffident fellow with a reputation for being a ladies man, Schiller (1860-1952), was born in Romania, earned a doctorate in chemistry and had been a top executive in a Berlin biochemical factory. He was lured to America by his homesick and pregnant sister Rose, who was married to Theodor Rosenfeld. Once in this country the Rosenfelds put the young biochemist to work managing the "Meininger" tour. After the tour's collapse, he acted as translator and escort for the legendary Eleanora Duse, whose 1893 American tour was handled by the Rosenfelds. It was widely rumored, and confirmed by Schiller during World War II, that the two were lovers. Later, Schiller would become manager and then husband of France's greatest singer, the legendary *diseuse* Yvette Guilbert (1868/69-1944) (Knapp 172-4).

But in 1892 Schiller was a 32 year-old recent immigrant with limited English and little practical theatre experience. His only qualification for *Intendant*, other than being Theodor Rosenfeld's brother-in-law, was that he reportedly had a good head for business (Milwaukee *Journal* 30 March 1892). He was in for a real donnybrook. The trouble actually began back in New York when Anna Haverland, one of the original Court Theatre actors who had been "specially engaged," rebelled against the European Meininger practice of actors alternating large and small roles (*New York Times* 13 Nov. 1891). When the troupe arrived in Philadelphia, she announced she would leave the company because, she said, "Parts do not afford me opportunities to display" (Philadelphia *Evening Item* 7 Jan. 1892; Meersman 43). By February she was appearing at The Amberg Theatre. Perhaps for similar reasons other performers, including Marianne Bedecovics and Gustav Rickelt (1862-1946), who in 1925 would be elected president of the International Actor's Union, dropped out in Cincinnati, St. Louis and Chicago. They were replaced by non-Meininger actors and German-speaking Americans.

Critical reaction to the "Meininger" continued to be somewhat favorable; the public, as it did in New York, stayed away. Of course, all the performances were in German and this may have reduced the "Meininger" to a novelty spectacle without established stars to all but German-speaking Americans. Regardless, the Rosenfelds were losing money and Schiller couldn't control his actors.

The first of two stops in Milwaukee temporarily boosted the company morale. Sixty percent of the city's 200,000 population spoke German. More than any other city in America, Milwaukee was dominated socially, politically and economically by German-speaking immigrants. Its mayor, Paul Bechtner, was a native of Stuttgart (Still 265). Yet curiously, not a single Milwaukee German language newspaper covered the events surrounding the "Meininger." What are we to make of this omission? By now the rumors of the scarcity of original State Court actors in the company had reached Milwaukee. Perhaps this ersatz troupe was a cultural embarrassment to the German community there. Whatever the reason, the failure of the Milwaukee German newspapers to chronicle the "Meininger" remains the tour's greatest mystery. The German-speaking reviewer of the Milwaukee *Journal* found that while the mob scenes in *Julius Caesar* were still fresh, the sets and properties had suffered from the wear and tear of constant touring. "It is probably true, the critic complained, "that many of last night's Roman citizens were probably born on the peaceful banks of the Milwaukee River, and had never strolled in the classic shades of Saxe-Meiningen," but

They were kept carefully in the background as "padding," and the front of the stage was occupied by some 20 or 30 "Supers" of both sexes of whom it is no exaggeration to say that they possess more inborn dramatic ability and thorough theatrical training than many Thespians playing important parts on our stage...The scenery is beautiful and effective, although some of it is noticeably shabby. The Capitol was furnished with everyday carpet. Some of the mob had boots which savored of Lynn, Massachusetts. (Milwaukee *Journal* 23 Feb. 1892)

The Milwaukee *Sentinel*, however, declared that the "Meininger's" staging was "surpassed only by Henry Irving" and the performance of *Julius Casear* "was exactly the kind of performance one expected from this company—no star, correct costumes, admirable stage setting" (Milwaukee *Sentinel* 22 Feb. 1892). The reviewers found the acting represented the finest the German theatre had to offer, except for the unfortunate Mathieu Pfeil (b. 1860), who "ranted" at times. But "all German actors," noted the *Journal*, "do that" (Milwaukee *Journal* 23 Feb. 1892). After four performances of *Julius Caesar* and *The Battle*, the

"Meininger" left Milwaukee for Chicago with seven railroad cars of scenery and properties. During its four-week Chicago engagement at the Grand Opera House, the troupe gave 32 performances, generally to mediocre reviews, of four plays, *Julius Caesar*, *The Battle*, Friedrich Schiller's *Mary Stuart* (*Maria Stuart*, 1800) and *The Robbers* (*Die Raüber*, 1781).

The "Meininger" returned to Milwaukee on March 27 and opened at Davidson's Theatre. After seeing *Mary Stuart*, the *Journal* critic no longer tolerated the "shabby" settings, suggesting that perhaps Schiller sold off some scenery while in Chicago.

It was, of course, pretty well known through the city that as far as the company was concerned there were very few of the Duke's players among them. But *Julius Caesar* and *The Battle*...with genuine scenery and properties, were not only in every particular based on the already artistically historical Meininger performances, but were in themselves historical in every way. Last night we were able to see modern Milwaukee furniture used on the stage by the "Meininger." Even the campstools were covered by Milwaukee carpet. (Milwaukee *Journal* 28 March 1892)

The hastily arranged setting wasn't the only failure in the new production. Marianne Bedecovics, who had rejoined the troupe in Chicago, was bitterly attacked. Noting that she hailed from a "small theatre in Berlin," the *Journal* remarked

She is probably the most desperate and determined ranter that has probably ever been seen on the boards in this city. She rants with everything—even her hair and veil. In other words, nearly all that she does is exaggerated and unnatural...The only facial expression at her command appears to be an ever-recurring frown and a droop of the lower lip that is not a natural combination or especially indicative of any particular human emotion. (Milwaukee *Journal* 28 March 1892)

The *Sentinel* was, if possible, even more personal: "Nature has not endowed Frl. Bedecovics to gratify this part. She has naturally a rather placid face, and she is not beautiful" (Milwaukee *Sentinel* 28 March 1892).

The production problems, however, were secondary to internal strife within the company. It all came to a head during the March 28 performance of *Mary Stuart* when *Intendant* Max Schiller physically attacked Gustav Kober (1849-1920), the troupe's leading actor. An argument over costumes erupted backstage and angry words passed between Kober, who had an explosive temper, and Schiller. The exasperated Kober told Schiller he was going to break his "Meininger" contract and return immediately to Germany. Schiller informed the rebellious actor that his contract was, according to the *Journal*, "cast-iron, copper-bottomed, steel- riveted," and he would take legal action if Kober attempted to leave. Kober retorted that a breach of a German contract could only be contested in a German court.[2] Then Schiller, according to eyewitnesses, called Kober a "lump" and made "a violent rush at the actor, who, by a dextrous movement of the body, protected himself from a blow." Both men "then closed and a lively catch-as-catch-can tussle followed. The noise from the fight was heard by the audience who could only imagine what the trouble was" (Milwaukee *Sentinel* 29 March 1892). After the curtain fell on the performance, Schiller refused to discuss the incident with newspaper reporters. "I don't see why I should," he said. "This is something that concerns the company only and no one else." A stagehand at Davidson's volunteered that "it was a pretty little fight for a moment, but nothing unusual. Such scraps occur whenever there is a German company playing here...they look more serious than they really are" (Milwaukee *Sentinel* 30 March 1892).

Serious or not, Schiller was arrested that night on charges of assault and battery and hauled off to jail. The next morning, accompanied by a lawyer and a translator, he stood before a Milwaukee municipal judge. The *Intendant*, who spoke "execrable English so that his opponents could not understand him," began his defense by telling the court that the company had been losing money and the actors were giving him trouble. He said that Kober's attempt to break his contract caused him so much pain that he had lost his head and struck him.

Stage manager Hilmar Knorr then testified against Schiller. Half the company, he boldly stated, were prepared to verify his testimony. He complained that Schiller provoked the actors, hoping they *would* break their contracts. Then Schiller could dissolve the troupe and avoid further debt. Other actors and stage hands, each of whom received an 83-cent witness fee, backed up Knorr's testimony.

Schiller gamely attempted a closing summation, but the presiding magistrate, Judge Wallber, had difficulty understanding him. The *Intendant* began by saying that he "loved his actors as children so that their ingratitude cut him to the core." He "thumped" Kober on the nose out of love for him, as Kober would "appreciate some day when he knew him better." Schiller carried on in this manner for some time until the impatient Judge Wallber finally stopped him, barking out, "Five dollars and costs!" "Herr Schiller," the *Journal* smugly noted, "will learn quickly that he cannot use his fists with impunity to handle his actors— at least in this country" (Milwaukee *Journal* 30 March 1892).

The next day, March 30, Schiller acted. He fired Kober, Mathieu Pfeil, and Hilmar Knorr, the latter two the only remaining members of the original Court Theatre. Schiller named himself stage manager. The mutiny was temporarily quelled, but the troupe had suffered irreparable loss. Kober and Pfeil were considered the company's finest actors. Christian Eckelmann replaced Kober as Franz Mohr in that night's production of *The Robbers* and the performance was a failure. "If he [Eckelmann] eliminates," the *Journal* remarked, "his excessive whispering and looking over his shoulder from his interpretation," he might make an actor someday. The unfortunate Eckelmann obviously hadn't time to learn his lines and blocking and was receiving instructions from a prompter. Other performers were upset by the dramatic turn of events. Bernard Weinkaus, heretofore a reliable actor, "played his part wretchedly." Years later Eckelmann would claim in his autobiography that his Franz Mohr was his best role with the American "Meininger," and he fondly recalled the "Thuringian bratwurst and Meininger beer" served on the "Meininger" tour train. As actors understandably are sometimes wont to do in a reminiscent mood, Eckelmann makes no mention of his Milwaukee debacle (Milwaukee *Journal* 1 April 1892; DeHart 51-2).

With the addition of *The Robbers* to the repertoire, the "Meininger's" careful attention to scenery disintegrated. The first two scenes in the play came from the Davidson Theatre's own stock, one setting was from *Mary Stuart*, and still another came from *The Battle* (Milwaukee *Journal* 3 April 1892).

The "Meininger" left Milwaukee on April 3, 1892, in shambles. They returned to New York and gave three desultory performances of *Mary Stuart* at the Academy of Music on April 8, 9 and 11. Adele

Sandrock (1864-1937), engaged for the lead role, refused to appear. She told the New York *Herald* that there was insufficient time to learn the difficult role, an unlikely excuse since Mary Stuart was her most famous part and she had performed it dozens of times (Carlson 195; Kosch 111, PT3, 1960). An inside source claimed Sandrock had a disagreement with the Rosenfeld Brothers. "In a huff," she declared she would not appear with the "Meininger." Her place was taken by Marianne Bedecovics, who this time "played the part acceptably" (New York *Herald* 8-9 April 1892).

Sandrock's quarrel with the Rosenfelds, like Anna Haverland's earlier rebellion, probably concerned billing. Throughout the American tour the company advertised itself as "The Meininger" and no individual actor was singled out for publicity. Sandrock, at age twenty-eight and one of Germany's leading actresses, might not have wanted to associate herself with the badly faltering pseudo "Meininger." Her hold-out was successful. The word "Meininger" never again appeared in the Rosenfeld publicity. During Sandrock's two week engagement she was supported by all the actors who survived the Milwaukee debacle (and who were probably still under contract), but they were no longer "The Meininger." The American "Meininger" tour had ended.

In retrospect, once the tour began unravelling, there was probably little that could be done to save it. Max Schiller was no Ludwig Chronegk. Years later, Max Grube, himself a onetime Court Theatre *Intendant*, realized the folly of an American tour without Chronegk. "If Chronegk had suddenly broken down in the middle of a tour of America," wrote Grube, "the consequences would have been incalculable; he was the soul and the moving spirit of everything" (Koller 102). Nowhere in his account of the Court Theatre does Grube mention this 1891-1892 "Meininger" troupe. The inexperienced Schiller, a continent away from home and operating without the authority of the Duke of Saxe-Meiningen, possessed neither Chronegk's patience with actors nor his artistic and organizational genius. Following the Schiller-Kober brawl, the actors struggled back to New York, found themselves in conflict with Adele Sandrock and the American "star" system, and were forced to discard their famous name. It was a sober ending for the actors and stagehands who had been members of the original Duke of Saxe-Meiningen Court Theatre.[3]

Part Three

Theatre in Small Town America

Chapter 7
"Left for Parts Unknown":
The Professional Stock Company
in Terre Haute, Indiana, 1857-58

Theatre historian Douglas McDermott argued in a 1978 essay that professional theatre on the nineteenth-century American frontier developed in three distinct chronological phases (McDermott 63-78). Phase one consisted of small troupes of itinerant actors and entertainers with little or no professional background. These vagabonds, like the Banvard company we saw in Chapter I, engaged in a variety of amusements and usually performed a limited play repertory in public buildings converted into theatrical spaces. During phase two, companies of perhaps two dozen professionally-trained actors and stagehands traveled extensively throughout the Ohio and Mississippi River Valleys, following the the major river systems—the Allegheny, Arkansas, Cumberland, Missouri, Ohio, and Wabash—and performed a repertory of two or three dozen plays in regular theatres. In the third phase, permanent stock companies with as many as twenty-four major actors performed in often elaborate urban theatres and produced perhaps four dozen plays per season.[1]

These third phase resident companies, notes theatre historian Seldon Faulkner, were the "mainstay of nineteenth-century American theatre, particularly in cultural outposts...far from the populous cities of the Northeast" (Durham 1, 346). A successful season required a "large and prosperous enough" (McDermott 68) city to support a full company and eliminate that company's need to travel. By the 1840s resident stock companies housed in permanent theatre buildings had been established in sizable population centers such as Pittsburgh, St. Louis, and Cincinnati by William Francis Courtney Wemyss, Benedict DeBar, and the team of Ludlow and Smith, among others.

But as late as the 1850s the smaller towns and villages in the river valleys, no longer a frontier of isolated and unconnected settlements, but a rapidly growing agricultural and manufacturing region, still had to make do with phase one and phase two travelling companies presenting second-rate dramas, crude farces and a variety of amusements. An anomaly, however, occurs mid-century in a small Indiana town called Terre Haute, justifying McDermott's warning that the evolution of frontier theatre was "not always as orderly as [my] theoretical model may imply" (McDermott 69-70).

Terre Haute, on the banks of the Wabash River, 70 miles west of Indianapolis and 110 miles north of New Harmony (see Chapter 1), was settled in 1810 by a farming co-operative led by Samuel Middleton and Peter Mallory (Bradsby 125). The area developed slowly despite the presence of a federal government fort and army detachment because of continued Indian hostilities and cholera epidemics between 1812 and 1820. Enoch Honeywell, a visitor to the village in fall of 1818, fell victim to cholera, took refuge in the crude fort and discovered that

The people are now sick more or less at every home in town...I think there are [*sic*] more than one person in ten throughout this settlement that escaped a siege of sickness this summer. Building, farming, and every other business has lain nearly idle since the middle of July [1817]. ("Diary of Enoch Honeywell," April 1818)

But a rapid growth, spurred on by the arrival in 1822 of the first steamboat and constant rumors that the new National Road would pass through, resulted in a sizable town that by 1823 had civic boosters taking pride in "fifty buildings!" and "a most splendid" court house and jail for a new county seat (*Western Register & Terre Haute Advertiser* 15 Oct. 1823). Most of those who settled in the still-swampy lands along the Wabash came from the East. A reunion of settlers in 1875 counted 124 among the 223 citizens present as natives of the Middle, Northeast and Atlantic states, 46 were born south of the Ohio River, nine individuals listed themselves as "foreign-born." All arrived in the area between the years 1818 and 1840 ("Old Wabash Valley Settlers Assoc. Minutes of 1875).

After 1830 the town established itself as an important manufacturing center. The National Road, which linked Baltimore with St. Louis and which was the major nineteenth-century migration route to the West, passed through the middle of town. The Wabash and Erie Canal, short-lived because of navigation problems on the Wabash (see Chapter 1), but vital for the town because of the workers it brought, and the Terre Haute-Richmond Railroad connected Terre Haute with the Great Lakes and the Eastern states respectively. By the late 1850s the town had a population of nearly 6,000 and all the trappings of modern civilization: thriving breweries, pulp mills, slaughter houses; a public library; one weekly and two daily newspapers; typically raucous Fourth of July celebrations; and a populace with a keen interest in cultural and civic affairs.

Terre Haute in the 1830s and 1840s attracted its share of circuses, novelty acts, minstrel shows, and concert singers. Amateur theatre, in a region where the most "lightly populated areas often developed amateur theatrical groups," apparently was nonexistent.[2] Although American critic Leman T. Rede declared "wherever immigration builds up a town or city, there rises a temple of drama," (Rede; qtd. Grimsted 49), professional performances of regular drama prior to 1857 were surprisingly rare, perhaps the result of a prohibitive $75 per performance theatrical license fee set by city ordinance. Few itinerant companies, if any, could have afforded such a fee for a one-night stand. The first advertised professional theatrical performance occurred on April 22, 1841, an improbably late date, when the MacKenzie and Jefferson Company asked for, and received, a reduction in the license fee and performed *The Brigand* and *The Spectre Bridegroom*. MacKenzie and Jefferson had experience at this sort of thing. While on tour in Springfield, Illinois, they persuaded the young attorney Abraham Lincoln to represent them in an attempt to overturn Springfield's heavy entertainment tax ("Minutes of the City Council Meetings 1840-41; Csida 38). Over the next several years, appearances were made by, among others, Herr Alexander, a magician and actor who gave away "$400 worth of jewelry," but who left town without paying his rent or his printing bills; the Wilkins and Mehen Company, which presented two weeks of plays; and the MacEvoy Family, featuring the Irish dwarf Mr. Allhead (Terre Haute, *Wabash Courier* 24 April 1841; *Daily Journal* 28 May 1852, 26 Aug. 1853, 28 Oct. 1853; *Wabash Express* 29 Dec. 1852).

Then, during the 1857-58 season Terre Haute, with little history of amateur or professional theatre, suddenly found itself with not one, but *two* resident professional stock companies. Two local businessmen, Samuel Dodson and Walker Hegeman, evidently felt that Terre Haute's population was large enough to support professional theatres. During a four-and-one-half-month period, the two men leased theatres, went to great lengths to form competent companies and produced a remarkable 114 different plays. In the end, hard pressed by ruthless competition, capricious actors and an agonizing wind-down to the season, the fledgling experiments failed. But for a brief period Terre Haute audiences savored a theatrical richness rarely known in the smaller Ohio Valley towns.

Samuel Dodson (1818-1890) was the son of a Scots Methodist frontier preacher and physician. Born and raised in West Tennessee, he had come to Terre Haute in 1854 to work on the Wabash and Erie Canal and the Terre Haute-Richmond Railway. Relatively young at 26, he already was recognized as a successful contractor when he leased Corinthian Hall in November 1857, and assembled Terre Haute's first resident stock company (Oakey 1, 322). Corinthian Hall, built in the early 1840s, occupied the middle floor of a three-story structure on the northeast corner of the town's Main and Third Streets. In a commercial arrangement common among Midwestern theatres, Jonas Strauss' grocery store was on the first floor, and the third floor housed a saloon and billiards parlor. J.M. Brown, Terre Haute's biggest theatre supporter, general town gadfly and gossip, and editor of the *Daily Union* newspaper, visited Dodson and his workmen and discovered that Corinthian Hall now housed "a large and handsome stage [and so] commodious a gallery in the upper end of the Hall that it is large enough to accommodate nearly twice the number of persons it formerly held...We expect a rush to Dodson's Theatre" (Hahn; *Terre Haute City Directory 1853* 146, *1858* 55; Terre Haute *Daily Union* 17 Nov. 1857).

Young Dodson assembled a talented, or at least experienced, company of itinerant actors and actresses, several of whom enjoyed long careers both on the frontier and in the larger Eastern theatre centers. The company included Bella Adams, Miss Julia Blake, Orlando W. Blake (b. 1832) and his wife, Julia Weston Blake (b. 1840); Thomas Cashman; Madame Francis; J.F. Lytton; Miss F. O'Harra, Mr. and Mrs. G.H. O'Harra; a Mr. Patterson; a Mr. Petmore; Miss T. Sawyer; Edwin N. Slocum (1836-95) and his wife, Mrs. E.N. Slocum; and T.P. Varney.[3]

A cursory look at the professional background of some of these actors reveals the restless, wandering life of the nineteenth-century entertainer. Bella Adams (sometimes Addams) appeared with her husband Charles F. Adams in Ludlow and Smith's company at the St.

Charles Theatre in New Orleans and in Mobile during the 1846-47 season. Three seasons later she was in New York where she co-starred with Mrs. J.W. Wallack, one of the great actresses of her generation, in a March 1850 production of *Pizarro*. Edwin N. Slocum, her leading man at Dodson's Theatre, also worked in New York, but mostly as a second-rank variety and character actor at Christy's Opera House and the Theatre Comique. T.P. Varney previously appeared in Terre Haute in 1853 with the Wilkins and Mehen Company. A former stage manager, he reputedly was "the most popular comedian" in Indianapolis. G.H. O'Harra, comedian and the company's musical director, performed with his wife, a comic actress, throughout the Ohio Valley with their O'Harra's String Band (Ludlow 660; Odell V, 537, VIII, 535, 644; *Daily Union* 22 Jan 1858, 23 Nov. 1857).

The life of these actors would have been hard, subject to the whims of managers and audiences, for by mid-century, the life of the American provincial actor had changed little from his or her counterparts in the earlier part of the century. William Dunlap, writing of actor John Martin, sadly noted that "he labored hard, lived poor, and died" (Dunlap 1, 171). It was an epitaph all too common for entertainers of the period. Edwin Forrest, who lived to the ripe old age of 66 and who was considered by his contemporaries the greatest native born American actor, bemoaned his "hateful, vagabond life...Such labour! God and the actor only know the fatigues of it!" (qtd. Grimsted 87-88). The salaries were low, the work strenuous. Rehearsing sometimes three plays at once during the day, actors then had to prepare for that night's performance. And, even if an actor had performed a role several times in other theatres, no guarantee ever existed that he or she had it memorized. The inability of stock performers to remember lines during performance was a common embarrassment (Grimsted 93).

Dodson's Theatre's first announced bill, on November 20, 1857, was *Loan of a Lover, Our Gal, and The Two Gregories* (*Daily Union* 21 Nov. 1857). The first two weeks ran smoothly with good-sized audiences and positive newspaper reaction. On December 1, the *Daily Union*, overlooking the more experienced actors, singled out a local variety entertainer for praise: "Some of the members of the company, who are all good, deserve particular notice, among whom Miss O'Harra stands pre-eminent...She is always up and never at fault" (*Daily Union* 1 Dec. 1857).

As Dodson worked feverishly to establish a foothold in the town, plans were under way for the opening of a second stock theatre, a remarkable occurrence in a place of such modest size. Walker Hegeman, a heavyset whiskey salesman in his mid 30s and who had moved to Terre Haute two years earlier, leased newly-built Carr's Hall, a two-story structure on the southwest corner of Walnut and Fourth Streets. The owner, Moses C. Carr, ran his grocery story on the first floor. The *Daily Union* reported on December 1, 1857, "The work of fitting up this fine Hall for theatrical purposes is rapidly progressing under the superintendence of Mr. William [sic] Hegeman, and the management of the accomplished artist engaged on the scenery. We happened by there yesterday and are much pleased with its appearance,—and a number of scenes have been hung" (*Daily Union* 1 Dec. 1857). None of the identities of the scenic artists who worked for Dodson and Hegeman survives. Were they itinerants, too? It seems likely. Newspapers often commented on the quality of the scenic values of the productions, and no evidence exists that any local artists were around who had the wherewithal to produce drops and settings for what would eventually mount to 114 different plays.

During the first week of January 1858, Hegeman traveled to Chicago and, probably through an agent, hired a number of actors for the season: George D. Chaplin (real name Inglis, b. 1837), Thomas L. Connor, Fanny Denham, Samuel Drake, Edward Lamb (1829-87) and his wife, Mrs. Edward Lamb; Harry Macarthy, Annie Radcliffe, Thomas B. Radcliffe (1812-1866), Dora Shaw, G.W. Shilling, Jerry Taylor, and C.H. Tyler. Later, when the theatrical wars were at their zenith, five actors from Dodson's company jumped to Hegeman's: Bella Adams, Mrs. Slocum, Mrs. Blake, Julia Blake, and J.F. Lytton.

Hegeman's actors, also itinerant troupers from the Western river system, brought with them considerable experience in frontier theatre. Samuel Drake, the most prominent name but hardly a prominent actor, was the son of Alexander Drake and the grandson of Samuel Drake, Sr., founder in 1812 of the first family acting troupe in the Old Northwest Territory. The younger Samuel apparently lacked the Drake Family talent, but he enjoyed a long career as a bit player, was always popular with Terre Haute audiences, and was one of the few actors there to receive his own benefit performance. Fanny Denham in 1855-56 performed at the New York Bowery Amphitheater and at Edwin L.

Davenport's innovative American Theatre. She came to Terre Haute from St. Louis, where she had been performing with Harry Macarthy. George D. Chaplin came directly from DeBar's Grand Opera House Stock Company in St. Louis, where he played juvenile roles. Englishman Thomas B. Radcliffe had immigrated to New Orleans in 1833, where he married (his wife did not accompany him to Terre Haute and the identity of Miss Annie Radcliffe hasn't been determined) and where he was a regular performer for several years. By 1852 he was a leading man at Cincinnati's National Theatre (Ludlow 304; Odell V, 201, 220; Smither 391; Wemyss 120).

Meanwhile, at the end of his first month of operation, Dodson was confronted with the first of many managerial problems. He was forced to close his theatre from December 22, 1857, until January 4 of the next year. The announced reason for the closing was the absence of the O'Harras who, abruptly and without explanation, left town (*Daily Union* 5 Jan. 1858). The two musical comedians may have received a promising engagement elsewhere, had a falling out with Dodson, or simply took a holiday for themselves. But they were the company's sole musicians and by all accounts popular with local audiences besides, and their absence apparently forced Dodson to darken his theatre during Christmas, the most financially lucrative period of the season. The O'Harras later returned, but perhaps out of spite, Dodson gave Mrs. O'Harra "third banana" roles where she languished behind other comic actresses the rest of the season. At any rate, the theatre re-opened on January 5 under a new title, "Dodson's Varieties," and a new hope.

Hegeman's stock company opened exactly one week later on January 12 with *The Toodles*, *A Kiss in the Dark*, and *Lady of the Lions*, a wildly popular burlesque of Bulwer-Lytton's *The Lady of Lyons*, America's most frequently produced drama at mid-century (Grimsted 254). Dodson had staged *The Lady of Lyons* on January 6. The Terre Haute theatrical wars had begun.

Bella Adams joined Dodson's Company on January 9 for a production of *Don Caesar De Bazan*. At her opening night intermission, she curried the favor of local audiences by delivering a passionate address to the city firemen, important resources in a century noted for disastrous theatre fires. After watching her performance, Editor Brown wrote," There is something new and peculiar, as well as interesting, in this lady's style which everyone should see and appreciate...but the supporting cast is poor" (*Daily Union* 11 Jan. 1858). Whatever her peculiarities and the weaknesses of the other actors, Adams used them to her advantage. She soon became the most popular actress in town.

Four days later Dodson introduced yet another lead actor, J.F. Lytton, an Irish comedian and vocalist. Lytton, with his engaging manner and broad Irish brogue, proved a hit among Terre Haute audiences. He sang, danced, performed comic afterpieces, and repeated his first production, *Limerick Boy*, four times over the next two months. Lytton's success resulted in Walker Hegeman going out and hiring *his* Irish comedian, Harry Macarthy. He also brought in Macarthy's current partner, Fanny Denham, to match Bella Adams. They opened together on January 29 in *Ireland As It Is*, *Irish Tutor*, and a "Grand National Tableau" in which Denham sang "The Star Spangled Banner" (*Daily Union* 29 Jan. 1858).

Dodson counterattacked with a lavish production of *Uncle Tom's Cabin*. At its opening on January 28, extra chairs were brought into Corinthian Hall to accommodate the overflowing crowd. Agelona Baugh, the daughter of Billy Baugh, a railroad engineer with a reputation as an eccentric local "character," played the pathetic Little Eva. The *Daily Union* remarked, "Considering the age of the little girl—some six or seven years—and the fact that she never before appeared on any stage, her rendition of the part was altogether creditable." The production, with several other local amateur actors, was repeated seven times with a Saturday matineé benefit for "schools and children" (*Daily Union* 29, 30 Jan. 1858). Shaw, an veteran Ohio Valley actress, opened at Hegeman's Theatre on February 3, 1858, with Sheridan Knowles' *The Hunchback*. After watching her later in *Ingomar the Barbarian*, Editor Brown could barely contain his excitement. Her performance "was a picture of life—such as would lead us to forget that it belonged to that little painted world, and by its perfection induce us to believe it rather a truth than a picture, a reality rather than a representation of an idea" (*Daily Union* 10 Feb. 1858).

Dora Shaw's engagement marked the high point of the season. Then things fell apart. The first blow fell on Sam Dodson the day after Shaw's debut when Bella Adams bolted his company on February 4 for Hegeman's Theatre to join Shaw in a production of *The Stranger*. Dodson's Varieties struggled on without its only certifiable local "star" for nine more days, in what was now obviously a losing cause, before closing for good on February 13, three and one-half months ahead of schedule. Manager Dodson then packed up most of his actors and scenery and headed south to Evansville, Indiana (*Daily Union* 25 Feb. 1858). Those actors left behind in Terre Haute hastily formed the Commonwealth Company, leased Corinthian Hall, and performed for their own "common wealth." Mrs. Blake took a benefit for herself in *Cabin Boy* and the next night T.P. Varney performed his own play, *Terre Haute Firemen*, for his benefit (*Daily Union* 19 Feb. 1858). These two benefits, the Commonwealth Company's only performances, suggest that Dodson fled abruptly, leaving behind some angry and unpaid actors that included Mrs. Slocum, Mrs. Blake, Julia Blake, and J.F. Lytton. These four then joined Bella Adams over at Hegeman's Theatre and continued performing there until the end of the season.

Hegeman's Theatre now supported a company of at least eighteen actors and, despite the absence of competition, limped toward the end of the season with apparently dwindling audiences. On February 16, in a rare display of Ohio Valley community support for the theatrical profession, the *Daily Union* published a letter praising Edward and Mrs. Lamb for their theatrical efforts and their contributions to the Terre Haute cultural scene. It was signed by thirty townspeople, including the city's mayor, C.Y. Patterson. The company in turn lavished praise—"in consideration of your gentlemanly, liberal, and unvarying conduct"—on their manager, Walker Hegeman, for a February 19 benefit in his honor. Hegeman wasted no time in accepting, for reasons that soon would become apparent. His biggest supporter, the *Daily Union*, noted that "Mr. H. [Hegeman] has certainly done everything within his power to establish a good and respectable theatre in this city."

He has engaged with considerable difficulty a company superior to any that has ever performed here. In all these respects he has entirely succeeded, although we regret to say his patronage has not been such as his efforts to establish a first class place of entertainment have merited. (*Daily Union* 16, 19 Feb. 1858)

Several of the actors left Terre Haute during the first week of March for Paris, a small Illinois town 32 miles distant, where they opened a one-month run. But Walker Hegeman and Dodson Theatre's Orlando Blake skipped out altogether, leaving in their wake a trail of unpaid bills,

Blake's teenaged wife, and the wrath of the *Daily Union*. One month after praising citizen Hegeman's "good and respectable theatre," the newspaper announced:

Blacklist

Walker Hegeman

A man of rather corpulent build, with full face, rather light hair, a sheepish look, about 35 years old, has left for parts unknown, and is indebted to us for $46 for job work. Said Hegeman has been in the whiskey business for the past two years, and undertook to establish a theatre here, but failed in the attempt and sloped with all the money he could raise...This man left many of our citizens in a worse fix than he did us.

Orlando Blake, described in his own "Blacklist" as having "hair on his face," was thought to be "hiding out" in Memphis, Tennessee, a logical deduction as a stock company was being formed there at a newly-constructed proscenium theatre, Memphis's first (*Daily Union* 19 March 1858; Durham 1, 345-46).

With Sam Dodson out of town and Walker Hegeman fled for "parts unknown," Bella Adams leased Corinthian Hall, launched her own company and tried to cash in on the good will she'd built up in the community: "In her opening prospectus she guarantees that nothing indelicate or obscene shall be permitted on her boards and declares her intention to present highly moral and Shakespearean dramas" (*Daily Union* 26 Feb. 1858).

Thus began the third major theatrical enterprise of the season. This troupe, recruited from the wreckage of the other two companies, included J.F. Lytton as stage manager, T.P. Varney, Fanny Denham, Mrs. Slocum, George D. Chaplin, Thomas B. Radcliffe, and the abandoned Mrs. Blake. In noting the formation of this new troupe, Editor Brown abruptly changed his tune. The failure of Terre Haute theatre was now the fault of the managers who didn't pay their bills and not the result of audience capriciousness.

The experience of the past three months—during which we have had two theatres open in our city, although they were conducted without experience or system, have [*sic*] proved conclusively that the project is feasible, and that the citizens of Terre Haute will support an establishment worthy of their patronage. (*Daily Union* 26 Feb. 1858)

Bella Adams's Theatre opened on February 26, 1858, with a production of *Six Degrees of Crime.* "The manner in which the new hall has been refitted," said the indefatigable *Daily Union,* "makes it decidedly pleasant and agreeable for both ladies and gentlemen. The most refined may now visit this theatre with propriety" (*Daily Union* 7 March 1858). Although she closed within the month, Adams produced plays fresh to Terre Haute audiences (*Damon and Pythias, Margaret Catchpole, Marie; or, The Daughter of the Regiment*) and true to her word, offered Shakespeare, perhaps furnishing a welcome relief to the repetitiveness of Dodson's and Hegeman's programs. The theatre darkened officially on March 24, with T.P. Varney in the title role of *Richard III.* The afterpiece, *Prairie Flower, or, The Hoosier Farmer,* was written by a "citizen of Terre Haute" (*Daily Union* 24 March 1858). In late March, the remnants of Hegeman's troupe returned from Paris, Illinois, and joined their fellow actors from the now defunct Bella Adams's Theatre. They gave two performances as the "Carr's Hall Troupe" on March 27 and 31 and then disbanded (*Daily Union* 27, 31 March 1858). The 1857-58 Terre Haute theatrical season had officially ended.

So what went wrong? Several things. The crucial period that sealed the fate of Dodson and Hegeman occurred between January 12 and February 11, 1858. In that one month span both theatres played on 26 consecutive performance nights and engaged in a cut-throat rivalry. Dodson brought in Irish comedian J.F. Lytton; Hegeman countered with Harry Macarthy and Fanny Denham. Dodson engaged Orlando Blake; Hegeman introduced Dora Shaw. Both managers needed solid financial backing to keep up this competitive pace and no evidence exists that they got it. In fact, the *Daily Union* implied that audiences dwindled significantly. It was only a matter of time before one or both went under. Despite the assortment of titles, productions at both theatres during this period offered theatergoers little choice, and the same play was often performed under two different titles, a common but still fraudulent theatrical practice of the period. J.F. Lytton appeared in his Irish farces, while Harry Macarthy appeared in his. On February 11, 1858, both theatres presented the same play, *Rough Diamonds,* while *Irish Tutor* was staged six times, *Lady of Lions* four times, and *Limerick Boy* four times.

The 114 plays staged were a mixture of standard pieces and a few new works that reflected resident company repertory in larger frontier and Eastern seaboard cities.[4] Eighteen distinct genres from burlettas to comic operas to tragedy are represented in their titles, and they were written almost entirely by British authors who in turn often plagiarized from their French counterparts. This is not a wholly unexpected occurrence as one modern researcher estimates a remarkable 50 to one ratio of imported drama to native drama existed in nineteenth century American productions (Rahill 225). What American plays were produced, such as Frances Brooke's *Rosina Meadows; or, Temptation Unveiled*, reputedly the first "full-blown American rural melodrama," were imitations of their British predecessors in form, style and substance (Rahill 258). The reasons for this "scarcity of native drama" are complex—theatre historian Bernard Hewitt appropriately called this period "growing pains"—and one student of the period has commented that "American plays, such as they were, came largely from hack journalists, actors, and theatre handymen—and amateurs" (*Theatre USA, 1668-1957*, Chapter 3; Grimsted 146). The "citizen of Terre Haute" who wrote *The Prairie Flower, or the Hoosier Farmer* was undoubtedly an amateur, T.P. Varney chipped in with his own *New York Firemen*, and enough American history tableaux, patriotic songs, sketches, volunteer fireman plays, "forest" plays (*The Forest Rose*, for example), and American rural and city dramas were produced to give a distinct American flavor to the Terre Haute season.

Two odd characteristics of the season's plays are immediately apparent. First, little Shakespeare was offered—two full length productions, *Romeo and Juliet* and *Richard III*, and two acts of a third, *Macbeth*. This paucity of Shakespeare, a mainstay of nineteenth century stock repertory, is somewhat puzzling. Perhaps the managers didn't have the scenic resources, the rehearsal time (most of the plays were short in duration), or enough actors to fully mount Shakespeare. The presentation of only the last two acts of *Macbeth*, an unusual production choice, certainly suggests that as a possibility. Second, the season offered more than its share of dated and hackneyed scripts; in fact, it was strikingly conservative compared to more adventurous stock companies in Memphis, Nashville, Louisville and St. Louis. Thirty-three of the plays, nearly one-third, had been staged *20 years* earlier in St. Louis during the 1837-38 season (Carson 326-27). Terre Hauteans were watching fare that was passé in most other Midwestern theatres.

As their titles often reveal, both dramas and comedies were concerned with four general themes: the romantic (*Loan of a Lover, Borrowing a Sweetheart, Wife for a Day, Maniac Lover*), the supernatural (*The Spectre Bridegroom, The Thumping Legacy*), the historical (*Charles II, Robert Emmett, La Tour De Nesle, William Tell, Don Casear De Bazan, Rob Roy*), and the domestic (*Margaret Catchpole, The Lottery Ticket, Rough Diamond, Pleasant Neighbor, Mr. and Mrs. White*). The presence of so many Irish comedians in town resulted in no less than 12 plays and several afterpieces with dominant Irish themes. The productions, chock-full of strong passions, mistaken identities, unhappy lovers, confidants, reversals, and disguises, featured physical action, and combat and they would have required large scenic pieces, whether or not the managers could provide them.

The season began to unravel when Bella Adams, who established a solid reputation in the town, deserted Dodson's Theatre for Hegeman's. Losing this popular performer must have been a severe setback for Dodson—he closed his theatre less than two weeks later. It was a delayed setback for Walker Hegeman as well, for not only did he offer free omnibus rides for reserved ticket holders, but he now had Harry Macarthy, Fanny Denham, Dora Shaw, and Adams, all frontier headliners, on his payroll (*Daily Union* 10 Feb. 1858).

Sam Dodson and Walker Hegeman appear to have begun the season in reasonably good financial shape, albeit probably with borrowed money. The refitted theatres reflected a certain civic pride in things cultural and both theatres began with excellent houses. The novelty, however, wore off, tensions undoubtedly mounted with defections and debts, attendance dwindled, and Bella Adams, who certainly caused enough problems by her own behavior, was left to pick up the pieces. Her season, even with its new plays and Shakespeare, was too short and too late and her early exit demonstrated further that the 1857-58 resident stock companies could not survive in a town the size of Terre Haute.

In the fall of 1858, T.P. Varney leased Corinthian Hall as "Varney's Gaieties" and opened, without any competition, on October 30 with C.B. Mulholland starring in *A Kiss in the Dark, Napoleon's Old Guard,* and the ubiquitous *Limerick Boy*. Admission was still 35 cents. The theatre

*with my hearts best love to
Fernando Flowery Harry Macarthy*

Fig. 5. Harry Macarthy. This Arkansas-born Irish comedian was a star of the 1857-1858 Terre Haute, Indiana, stock season. At the outbreak of the Civil War, Macarthy penned "The Bonnie Blue Flag," the Confederacy's official national anthem. *Harvard Theatre Collection.* Reprinted with permission.

was, noted the *Daily Union*, "still affording a pleasing place of resort, which is far better for our young men than running around the city spending twice the admission"[5] Varney's Gaieties abruptly folded less than three weeks later and Varney returned to Indianapolis to continue his career. With his departure the professional stock company in Terre Haute died. Future professional theatre in the town consisted of traveling companies with major stars performing limited engagements (see Chapter 8).

Other veterans of the 1857-58 Terre Haute theatre wars dispersed and most returned to their former itinerant lives. Bella Adams left town with a new husband in tow and opened a theatre in Evansville, Indiana. Fanny Denham's experience apparently soured her on frontier theatre. By 1862 she was back in New York City where she stayed for the rest of a long and relatively distinguished career as a character actress. George D. Chaplin later performed in Chicago and later still in New York, where he worked with America's most prominent actors, including John E. Owens and Lawrence Barrett. His travels in 1872 took him to the West Coast as leading man for the San Francisco California Stock Company, and the next season he stage managed at DeBar's Grand Opera House, St. Louis, returning to the stage where he began his career back in 1857, and where he was joined by Thomas L. Connor. Thomas Radcliffe worked as a stage manager in New Orleans. Samuel Drake retired to a Louisville, Kentucky, farm owned by his grandfather. The Lambs moved East and by 1871, Edward was the manager and leasee of New York's prosperous Park Theatre. Edwin N. Slocum, whose future relationship with his wife isn't known, left the legitimate stage to become a black-faced minstrel performer, eventually managing his own highly successful troupe.[6]

Harry Macarthy, billed as a genuine Irish performer, was actually born and raised in Arkansas. Despite Hegeman's patriotic tableaux, which included "The Star Spangled Banner," Macarthy's patriotism had a decidedly Southern bias. Three years after leaving Terre Haute he wrote the words and music to "The Bonnie Blue Flag," the offical national anthem of the Confederacy. Only "Dixie" rivaled it as the South's most popular Civil War song. In 1861, the *Wabash Express* informed its Terre Haute readers that Dora Shaw was playing Camille to packed houses at Cincinnati's Pike's Opera House. Samuel Dodson left the theatre business for good and entered a long life of public service as an elected official. Before his death in 1890, he served three terms as Terre Haute's city tax collector, one term as its marshall, and one term as its street commissioner (Heaps 54-55; *Wabash Daily Express* 24 Dec. 1861; Oakey 322). Walker Hegeman's later activities are unknown, but then, there was never a shortage of whiskey salesmen in the nineteenth-century Midwest.[7]

Chapter 8
A Stop on the "Proximical" Tour:
Edwin Booth in Terre Haute

In 1873, the residents of Terre Haute, Indiana, now far removed in spirit, if not years, from the rough and tumble days of its 1857-1858 stock season, couldn't wait to show their visiting star Edwin Booth the wonders of the town's new cultural institution, The Grand Opera House. For Edwin Booth it was just another payday in small-town America, part of a Midwestern tour to raise money to save his New York Booth's Theatre from impending bankruptcy. It was a scene played out all across the Midwest during the last quarter of the century, as towns built ornate theatres, called them "grand opera houses"—proving, at least to themselves, that, having tamed the frontier, they were now just as civilized as residents on the Eastern Seaboard—and invited prominent theatrical stars to perform in them. But something happened when Edwin Booth came to town, something uncomfortable and embarrassing for its residents, for Booth appeared on stage on the anniversary of his brother John Wilkes's assassination of Abraham Lincoln. The ambivalent reaction of Terre Hauteans to his performances makes for an interesting story.

By the early 1870s Terre Haute was a bustling, thriving community of 10,000 people, its distilleries and pork and brick industries bolstered by the presence of the Terre Haute-Indianapolis Railroad and the National Road. More often than not, however, collective civic pride was directed toward the town's cultural and artistic achievements. Its emerging cultural consciousness was typical of growing communities, demonstrating, as historian Neil Harris has observed,

The zeal of residents in publicizing their home cities as places deserving outside respect (and patronage) because of their cultural amenities. Literary societies and academies were advantages alongside convenient railroad lines and fine harbors. Guidebooks and newspapers...presented their panoply of institutions as

113

proof of urbanity and wealth." (Harris "Four Stage of Cultural Growth" 31)

Terre Haute's 1868-69 *City Directory* praised the town's "excellent churches, academies, and our cultural fineries" (*Terre Haute City Directory 1868-1869*). But, according to the civic fathers and the local newspapers, including the *Daily Union*, champion of the 1857-1858 stock season, one component was missing among the "cultural fineries." Terre Haute didn't have its own large, opulent theatre like its larger sister cities Cincinnati, Louisville, St. Louis, Indianapolis, or even many smaller towns in the Ohio Valley. Small, cramped and dowdy, Dowling Hall, the town's one theatre at the time, was adequate, but far from impressive for a forward-looking city that wanted to attract the big stars of the day.

In 1870 several local businessmen pooled their financial resources, borrowed money from a New York City bank, and built The Grand Opera House in the heart of the town's business district at Fourth Street and Wabash Avenue. Designed by the prominent architect J.A. Vrydagh, and featuring interior murals painted by Robert Buckels (1842-1914), an English artist later knighted by Queen Victoria, it was indeed "grand." But it came at a steep price. The theatre's construction was budgeted at $60,000, but, as often happens when committees plan buildings, the eventual costs rose to slightly more than $178,000 (Oakey 1, 324).[1]

The Grand opened on December 18, 1870 with a production of *Everybody's Friend*, with John E. Owens, veteran comedian and one of the country's most popular actors (Terre Haute *Journal* 19 Dec. 1870).[2] The next day the Indianapolis *Journal* remarked, "Suffice it now to say, that the Grand is first-class in all respects, both as to constructions and appointments, ranking it with the best public halls in the West—or, indeed, the country anywhere" (Indianapolis *Journal* 20 Dec. 1870). By its third season, 1872-1873, the Grand Opera House became what Terre Hauteans had envisioned—a showcase for the most prominent theatrical stars and personalities of the day. Laura Keene (c. 1820-1873), in her final year on the stage; Dan Rice (1823-1900); Lotta Crabtree (1847-1924); Mrs. George C. Howard (1818-87) of *Uncle Tom's Cabin* fame, and Bidwell and MacDonough's production of *The Black Crook*, the notorious musical featuring scantily-clad women, all took the stage at the Grand during the season. But the premier attraction, the one that caused the greatest excitement, was Edwin Booth.

Fig. 6. Edwin Booth (1833-1893), America's most famous actor in Hamlet, his most famous role. *Walter Hampden-Edwin Booth Collection, The Players*. Reprinted with permission.

Edwin Thomas Booth (1833-93) is arguably the greatest actor in American theatre history. His contemporaries certainly thought so. "We of today live in the era of Booth," declared the New York *Evening Post* in 1870, and at his death he was something of a national cultural institution. While he modestly claimed he was practicing "the only trade for which God has fitted me," his "pre-eminence...was unquestioned" (qtd. Shattuck xiii, 274, 53). He founded the famous Players Club in New York City, in front of which his statue stands today, worked diligently to raise the social status of theatre folk, and poured his talent and craft into an astonishing variety of roles at home, in England—where he appeared with Henry Irving at Irving's Lyceum—in Germany and in exotic places like Hawaii and Australia. But Booth reached this exalted status through pain, perhaps a touch of madness, and a tragic family history that Booth once described, in one of his more cheerful moods, as, "We've had some ups and downs" (Kimmel 382).

Edwin was the second surviving son of Junius Brutus Booth, Sr. (1796-1852). Junius, the son of a London barrister, was by all contemporary accounts a brilliant, bombastic and erratic actor, who by 1818 had established himself as a rival to Edmund Kean, England's best tragedian. Then in 1821, the quixotic Junius, who always exhibited a restless nature, inexplicably deserted his legal wife Adelaide, in a theatrical act if there ever was one, for a lowly Bow Street flower girl named Mary Ann Holmes. The two lovers sailed to a new life in America, where Junius toured the provinces and received favorable critical notices in New York. He and Mary Ann had ten children, six of whom survived into adulthood, and in 1851, a scant year before Junius's death, Adelaide finally agreed to a divorce. After 30 years the fugitive lovers finally wed.

If talent is a flame and genius a fire, Junius Booth was a roaring volcano on the stage. But half-mad, eccentric in the extreme, he lived his offstage life in such a rush of excess that as early as 1829 a Boston newspaper called him "a lunatic of the first water." In December of that year he walked off the stage of Boston's Tremont Theatre during the performance of an afterpiece called *Amateurs and Actors*. He began this particular tirade by stepping up to the footlights and laughing, then insanely cackling, at the audience. As the stage manager dragged him away, he shouted "I can't read,—I am a charity boy;—I can't read. Take me to the Lunatic Hospital!" That was just the beginning of a steady downward spiral into madness and strong drink that led his biographer, for understandable reasons, to refer to him as "The Mad Tragedian" (Kimmel 47-48).

Edwin Booth, raised on the Maryland family farm, appeared with his father at an early age. By 1850 he was trouping the Eastern seaboard with Junius, establishing a pattern the two would follow until the elder Booth's death in 1852. In April of that first year, during a New York City benefit performance of *Richard III* for Master Murray, an infant phenomonen who "had taken the fancy of the public" (see Chapter 4), Junius, whether drunk, obstinate or genuinely angry at having to co-star with a child, refused to leave his hotel room and go to the theatre. "Go play it yourself!" he shouted at his 17-year-old son. So Edwin did, apparently to great effect, making his stage debut in a major role which he had not even rehearsed (Kimmel 76, 77).

Then in 1851, character actor Augustus W. Fenno (1815-1873), recently back from the California Gold Rush, convinced Junius that vast riches awaited actors who worked the gold fields and the burgeoning city of San Francisco. So Junius and Edwin headed for California, where the son became father to the man. Edwin filled a thankless watchdog role, cleaning up after Junius following his drunken sprees, dealing with his father's numerous sexual liaisons, and smoothing things over with managers when Junius caused trouble. It was an intense experience for an always sensitive young Edwin, trouping and nursemaiding this unpredictable, mercurial, larger-than-life actor, but by now, according to his mother, he had "learned many of his father's tricks and usually could control him." In November 1852, Junius, halfway through a trip back East without Edwin (he had stayed behind in San Francisco), caught pneumonia and, confused and lost without the care of his son, died on a steamboat just outside Louisville (Kimmel 84).

Edwin, free from the stifling presence of and responsibilities toward his father, began a slow but inevitable climb to the top of his profession. But the memories of those touring years never left him. All his life he lived in fear that he, too, was touched with madness, a fear that intensified when his younger brother John Wilkes (1839-1865) assassinated Lincoln. Edwin, an intelligent man but certainly no intellectual, possessed an "earnest, unaffected personality" and was generous to friends and foes alike (Shattuck xxvi). But he was moody and frequently depressed, fretting at things that might seem trivial to another under the same circumstances. On the other hand, Booth had some cause for bouts of depression. His personal life, in a century that sentimentalized early death, seems almost more than one could bear. His first wife, Mary Ann, died at 22, his second, Mary McVicker, at 33, his brother John Wilkes at 27. Two sisters and a brother died the year Edwin was born. Of illegimate birth, both blessed and cursed with a genius for a father—no wonder Richard Lockridge titled his popular biography of Booth *Darling of Misfortune* after an utterance of Booth's, when, having lost a treasured good luck charm late in life, the superstitious actor remarked, "I knew my luck would turn. Misfortune came. I think few have had more" (New York: Century Co., 1932; Kimmel 333).

Was Edwin, like his father, tinged with madness? Probably not. But his own questioning of his mental stability appears to have shown up in his acting. In fact, some have seen him as using his uncertainty about his mental status as a tool, that, like the modern neurotic "method" actor, propelled him to the edge, that created the "look" which mesmerized his contemporaries during performance and which still, 130 years later, hauntingly stares out at the modern viewer from old photographs. His desertion of his father and Junius's subsequent death affected his entire career. Historian Richard Cohen, in an arguable statement, goes so far as to say, "The secret of Booth's performance was that while he played Hamlet as sane, he himself, in a manner of speaking, was mad. His madness gave the performance its edge" (Cohen 53-54). There may be some truth to this. Charles Shattuck, a leading Booth scholar, believes that Booth prepared for the role of Hamlet like no other, and the play's theme, "a living son seeking a dead father, became for Booth almost an autopsychography." And, added to that was the fierce determination of nineteenth century audiences to identify Booth *as* Hamlet. His contemporary Laurence Hutton wrote that "in many minds Booth *is* Hamlet...any picture of Hamlet which does not resemble the familiar features of Booth, any representation of Hamlet on stage which is not an imitation of Booth's Hamlet, is considered no Hamlet at all" (Shattuck 5; Hutton 294).

Booth's talent reached its zenith in 1864 when, in an unprecedented run, he played *Hamlet* 100 consecutive performances at New York's Winter Garden Theatre. Then came the Lincoln assassination. Booth was arrested and detained, and the rest of his family suffered greatly, as one might well imagine. He went into retirement, but returned triumphantly with a New York production of, naturally, *Hamlet* on January 3, 1866. When the Winter Garden burned, Booth fulfilled a lifelong dream by building his own theatre, Booth's Theatre, on the corner of Sixth Avenue and Twenty Third Street. Its first season in 1869 was a great success, offering, Booth thought, "the finest actors in the best of classic and modern drama" (Shattuck 66). Late in the season Kate Bateman, now a mature woman and a prominent actress, appeared in *Leah the Forsaken* and *Mary Warner* (see Chapter 4). Finally, after being tempered on the forge of frontier theatre and after devoting 20 hard years to his craft, he felt secure. That same year he married Mary McVicker, step-daughter of Chicago's J.H. McVicker, the Midwest's most prominent theatre owner and manager of the tour that landed Booth in Terre Haute.

Then, as happened in so many instances when Booth's life seemed stable and fulfilled, it all came crashing down. In 1870 Edwin and Mary McVicker's first child, Edgar, died within a few hours of birth. Mary fell into a deep depression, the first signs of mental instability and generally poor health that plagued her, and Edwin, until her death in 1881. Then three years later the Financial Panic of 1873 wiped out Booth's Theatre. The theatre's profits since its opening were reportedly high, but its income steadily dwindled each successive season and by January 1873, when signs of a national financial depression first became apparent, Booth's liabilities were staggering. He owed his creditors over $300,000. Edwin persuaded his brother Junius, Jr. to take over theatre temporarily, hoping that this release from managerial responsibilities would free him to undertake a whirlwind tour of undetermined length to pay off his huge debt. But personal problems still distracted him. Mary McVicker Booth was seriously ill. Never a strong woman, her nerves shattered by her first pregnancy, Mary's health had further weakened after the birth of their daughter Edwina in 1861. She suffered a relapse during the winter of 1872-1873 (Lockridge 212).

As Booth prepared for his tour and before the creditors moved in, a strange incident took place at Booth's Theatre. The affair, even if it is, as I suspect, apocryphal, nevertheless gives us an insight into the state of Booth's mind prior to his Terre Haute appearance. Gerrie Davidson, who did odd jobs around the theatre, said that in early February, just prior to the tour, Booth gave him orders to be awakened at three o'clock in the morning. Early the next day, after Davidson had done as he was told, Booth led him downstairs to the furnace room below the Booth Theatre stage. He gave directions to Davidson to stoke the furnace while he, Booth, opened a large trunk with an ax. Inside the trunk were several tightly-packed costumes. Booth took out the costumes one by one and, after carefully inspecting each article, handed it over to Davidson with instructions to burn it. There in the early morning, with the eerie glow of the furnace around them, Davidson recognized the costumes' owners by their initials. They belonged to Booth's father Junius and his brother John Wilkes (Ruggles 241).

Booth's 1873 Midwestern tour, born of financial desperation, burdened the actor with a sickly and unstable wife, lingering memories of a tragic family background, and an uncertain future. More trouble was on the way. In early February he launched his tour with an extended run at his father-in-law's theatre, McVicker's, in Chicago. Most of his supporting company was taken ill. Six weeks prior to his Terre Haute appearance, illness claimed the life of Augustus Fenno, his father's old friend and the man who first suggested the 1851 California tour. Fenno played "dignified old men's parts," including the Second Actor in Edwin's 1870 run of *Hamlet*, and was one of Edwin's beloved links to his past. Walter Joyce, another old friend of Booth's and a supporting actor, also died (Grossman 36; Shattuck 87).

On April 10, beset by these personal problems and accompanied by a less than healthy company, Booth arrived in Terre Haute from Lafayette, Indiana. The *Daily Express* ran but one extravagant ad (Terre Haute *Daily Express* 10 April 1873),

TWO NIGHTS ONLY
April 10th and 14th
Under the management of Mr. J.H. McVicker,
Manager of McVicker's Theatre in Chicago
Thursday Evening, April 10th
The Eminent Actor, Mr.
Edwin Booth
In his great Shakespearean character of
HAMLET

Monday Evening, April 14
As the Cardinal, in Bulwer's great historical
play of
RICHELIEU

Supported by a full Dramatic company selected from Booth's Theatre, New York, and McVicker's Theatre, Chicago, and present with the same Costumes, Properties, and Appointments as used during the great run of the pieces at Booth's Theatre, New York

$1.50 First row, front family circle
1.00 Family Circle
.50 Gallery

Several excursion groups from the surrounding area came by train to watch the performance of *Hamlet*. The Indiana towns of Greencastle, Sullivan, Brazil, and Paris, Illinois, all sent official delegations. People were literally falling over themselves; on April 11, the Terre Haute House, the town's leading hotel, announced that it had served supper to 198 people in its already crowded dining room in addition to its "regular" list of patrons (Terre Haute *Daily Express* 11 April 1873).

As one might expect, *Hamlet* was enthusiastically received. It was, after all, Booth's greatest role, although he also excelled in other Shakespeare roles—Iago, Othello, Shylock. His 1870 New York Hamlet, said a respected critic, was "a genuine feast of reason, of beauty...of histrionic intelligence and splendor," for Booth forsook the bombastic stage fury made popular by Edwin Forrest (1806-1872), his own father and his brother John Wilkes. Instead he concentrated on the gravity of the character, investing Hamlet with deliberate movement and action and creating a picture of studied naturalness. Although certainly not without his critics—he was accused of "an unpleasant habit of sinking the head between the shoulders, *crouching* as it were"—most viewers found it "America's Hamlet" and they gloried in it. His provincial tours of *Hamlet* provoked applause that was "instaneous, electrical, universal" (Shattuck 69, 90). Terre Hauteans reacted to his performance in much the same manner. A survey of the local newspaper reviews and comments on the production reveal in interesting ways the prevailing theatrical tastes of the period. The editor of the *Evening Gazette*, an avid theatergoer who had to push and shove people aside to find his seat, commented,

Mr. Booth's rendition of this singular character of Shakespeare's wonderful creation, certainly more nearly approximates perfection that that of any other actor. From the time he appears on stage, his fine form and the grace of his actions are firmly fixed in the minds of those of his auditors who can appreciate the highest histrionic talent. His support was better than the average of traveling companies. (Terre Haute *Evening Gazette* 11 April 1873)

Not everyone agreed that the company was "better than average." The *Evening Mail* noted that "Edwin Booth is so grand an artist that he draws immense houses, despite the hindrance of a weak company and the much more serious drawback of an inefficient manager." While the paper didn't elaborate on the "inefficient manager"—he may not have paid the printing bills— it was probably correct in its estimation of the supporting company. Booth often was criticized for tolerating poor actors around him because he realized that audiences came to see him, not the other players, and his companies were either "reasonably good or very bad" (Terre Haute *Saturday Evening Mail* 12 April 1873; Shattuck 83). The charge is tempered by the fact that nearly all the prominent actors of the period were accused of the same thing; it was, after all, the age of the star in the American theatre.

And what a star he was! Booth cut a striking figure as Hamlet. Dressed completely in black, with leggings crisscrossed with pink cloth strips and an undershirt with striped sleeves, he commanded the stage despite his average height. Around his neck he wore a chain from which hung a locket containing a miniature, ostensibly of Hamlet's father. Edwin kept a picture of *his* father in the locket and it stayed there for his entire career (Shattuck 124).

The rest of the critics in Terre Haute were fulsome in their praise of *Hamlet* and reluctant to write anything that might strike their visitor as negative criticism. One writer didn't even feel the necessity of commenting on the performance: "His rendition of the familiar role of Hamlet was witnessed with intense delight. So many thousand descriptions of Booth's Hamlet have been written that the subject may be considered exhausted" (Terre Haute *Daily Express* 11 April 1873). Other critics demonstrated the same reluctantance.

Without unnecessary blowing and no extra amount of advertising, Edwin Booth attracted at the Opera House on Thursday evening one of the finest audiences ever assembled in that building. Every seat was filled from the orchestra to the upper gallery with many gentlemen standing against the walls. This is real fame! Of Booth's Hamlet—We should as soon think of painting a rainbow as to describe it. So perfect in every word, every gesture, every movement. In this impersonation he has no equal on the American stage. (Terre Haute *Saturday Evening Mail* 12 April 1873)

A woman correspondent from Paris, Illinois, commented on Booth's death scene, one that the actor had constantly embellished since 1870, eventually producing his "Oh, I die, Horatio" line in a "supremely pathetic" manner but keeping "at all times a harmony of action and posture." The Paris commentator wrote from a distinctly romantic point of view, emphasizing the feminine aspects of Booth's treatment of the character.

It needs no art to make Booth look Hamlet. The high forehead crowned with long black hair; the magnificent rolling eyes, the tender mouth, sensitive in its play as a woman's, the lithe, sinewy form, full of infinite grace, are essentially the property of Hamlet. Woe betide the men if those eyes were in a woman's head, and she possessed the same powers, for her victims would number in the thousands. When he weeps, he uses his handkerchief, drying his face as a woman does. Then he dies as a woman dies—not with the strong agony of a man; simply the throwing back of the head, with one or two convulsive gasps, a slight quivering of the limbs, and the white face is set. (Shattuck 280; Terre Haute *Evening Gazette* 15 April 1873)

It's a wonder the critics could see or hear the production. In an act that showed Terre Hauteans were not as far removed from their frontier days as they would liked to have believed, the audience exhibited unruly, rowdy behavior. The normal seating capacity of the Grand Opera House was 1,400. Standing room would have raised that figure to 1,700 or 1,800, so the place was certainly overcrowded. An angry patron wrote the *Evening Gazette*, "There were some people at the Opera House last evening who failed to see anything to admire except the witticisms put into the mouth of the old gravedigger. While they could not enjoy the entertainment, they seemed determined that those who could, should not, and so they whispered and laughed and rustled programs during the performance." Others were equally disgruntled. The anonymous "N.B.R." complained,

The Terre Haute audience, as they always do when they have anything really fine at the Opera House, waited to array themselves finely and kept coming in all during the first and second act, to the great annoyance of those who were there to see the play; as if they fully expected someone to look at them, when Booth was playing Hamlet on the stage before them. At the close, before Hamlet was fairly dead, or the curtain had fallen, they rose up en masse and started from the house. (Terre Haute *Evening Gazette* 11 April 1873)

Booth and his company left for Evansville, Indiana on Saturday, April 12, and—this schedule must have been exhausting—they returned to the Grand Opera House on April 14, a Monday, for a performance of Lord Bulwer Lytton's *Richelieu*. But *Richelieu* drew only three short comments in the Terre Haute newspapers, no reviews were printed, and hardly anybody came to the play. And therein lies a mystery. Cardinal Richelieu, Booth's favorite role after Hamlet, was a sure-fire crowd pleaser, all "melodrama and flashy histrionics." Audiences, in era in which the lines between popular and "high" art were indistinct, considered Lord Bulwer-Lytton (1803-1873), a playwright whose turgid works are almost never produced today, as nearly Shakespeare's equal and *Richelieu* as "an unequaled gem in the player's art" (Shattluck 39). The editor of the *Saturday Evening Mail* complained that on the Saturday before *Richelieu* he had to wait a full hour in the lobby of the Grand to buy his ticket. Booth had a "fine" audience, but its size was embarrassingly small compared to the one for *Hamlet* (Terre Haute *Saturday Evening Mail* 19 April 1873). So where did the audience go? Three reasons might account for the apparent disinterest in *Richelieu* after the excitement generated by *Hamlet*: the audience was small because heavy rains had fallen during the previous weekend, the audience had seen Booth as Hamlet and, in doing so, satisfied their curiosity, and, more intriguingly, *Richelieu's* performance date, April 14, was the anniversary of the Lincoln assassination.

Heavy rains did indeed fall during the weekend after *Hamlet* and before *Richelieu*. The Wabash River rose so quickly that town officials feared it would flood and contaminate the water works building located hard by the river bank a mere three and a half blocks from the theatre, a fact which the *Evening Gazette* blamed for the poor turnout (Terre Haute *Daily Express 12 April 1873; Evening Gazette* 15 April 1873). But if the weekend downpour was responsible, why did the editor of the *Saturday Evening Mail* complain about the long wait for his ticket on Saturday morning when the storm was at its peak? "The sale of seats," he commented, "indicate [sic] another grand ovation awaits him" (Terre

Haute *Saturday Evening Mail* 12 April 1873). That same Saturday night, despite the inclement weather, two theatrical troupes played to full houses—the Sappho Opera Company at the Grand and a circus staked out on First Street (Terre Haute *Journal* 14 April 1873; *Evening Gazette* 14 April 1873). Ticket sales were brisk for *Richelieu,* people turned out to see other amusements, and yet the audience was small for Booth's second appearance.

Delegations from various Western Indiana and Eastern Illinois communities had come to see *Hamlet.* They stayed the night at various hotels and then returned to their hometowns. Some Terre Hauteans, if the audience behavior is any indication, were at the *Hamlet* performance for social reasons. But even taking into account the absence of these novelty seekers on the night of *Richelieu,* it seems reasonable to assume that enough interested patrons were left in a town of 10,000 people to provide the Grand with a full house on Booth's second night.

The third reason is the more intriguing. April 14, 1873, the date of the *Richelieu* performance, was the eighth anniversary of Abraham Lincoln's assassination by John Wilkes Booth. Indiana had played a prominent role in securing Lincoln's nomination for the presidency in 1860 (Roll 1-13). Terre Haute herself took pride in Lincoln's Indiana childhood and overwhelmingly supported him during the presidential campaigns of 1860 and 1864. Also, her citizens paid an unusually high price during the Civil War; fully one-fifth of the town's population, 2,003 men, served in the northern armies, and the casualty rate was high. As late as 1891, 45 percent (228 of 500) surviving Terre Haute veterans were permanently disabled (Bradsby 449).

A political link also existed among owners and editors of Terre Haute newspapers and Abraham Lincoln. Major General Charles Cruft, staunch Republican, prominent Civil War veteran and owner of the *Express* until April of 1872, was a personal friend of Lincoln's. He and Colonel R.N. Hudson, owner and editor of the *Journal,* served as marshals during Indiana's segment of the Lincoln funeral procession from Washington to Springfield, Illinois. These men were influential Terre Haute citizens and, according to contemporary published reports, devoted to Lincoln and to his memory (Oakey 1, 309). All the Terre Haute newspapers carried articles and memorials concerning Lincoln's death on April 14, 1872 and April 14, 1874. But on April 14, 1873, with Edwin Booth in town, and perhaps embarrassed by his presence and the

Fig. 7. Terre Haute, Indiana's Grand Opera House as it appeared in 1873. *Author's Collection.*

clash between bitter memory and cultural attainment, none of the papers mentioned Lincoln's name at all, as though any mention of the assassination would have been considered painful for the visiting star. But here was the assassin's brother appearing on the anniversary of the president's death in, of all places, a theatre.

The fact the Lincoln was shot in a theatre had a profound effect on the American stage at the time. Dozens, perhaps hundreds, of theatres were forced to close down; some actors, including Edwin Booth, were arrested and held without charge; and the nation's Protestant community, as it had throughout the century, roundly denounced the theatrical profession with renewed vigor. The Rev. Phineas D. Gurley, Washington, D.C., thundered, "Let it [the theatre] stand for years to come as it now stands, silent, gloomy, forlorn, more like a sepulcher than a place of amusement, saying to all passersby, 'Here the greatest crime of the age was committed by one who was addicted to tragedy and made the stage his home'." The Rev. Justin Dewey Fulton of Boston told his flock that Lincoln "did not die on Mt. Nebo, with his eyes full of heaven. He was shot in a theatre. We are sorry for that. It is a poor place to die in." "Would Mr. Lincoln had fallen elsewhere," a Rev. Duffield of Detroit was quoted as saying, "than at the very gates of Hell—in the theatre" (qtd. Sandburg 357-59). It would be interesting to discover sermons delivered by Terry Haute clergymen the day before the Monday performance of *Richelieu*. Did they discourage their parishioners from attending the Grand Opera House?

The result of all this is that Lincoln's death wasn't mentioned, *Richelieu* received scant attention in the newspapers, and the public, with the assassination still fresh in its mind, stayed away from the one symbol of its civic pride—the Grand Opera House. During his absence in Evansville, Booth received a strange public apology from the *Express*. Earlier in the week the paper had noted that "McVickers [*sic*] of McVicker's in Chicago, is managing Booth on his proximical tour." An embarrassed editor explained, "Edwin Booth was astonished yesterday to find himself on a 'proximical' tour, sent there by a fastidious printer who didn't like the word provincial" (Terre Haute *Daily Express* 13 April 1873). No town with a magnificent opera house and a visiting star the magnitude of Edwin Booth could be considered, in any form of the word, "provincial."

Edwin Booth's Midwestern tour failed to save his theatre. The events of the Panic of 1873 were overwhelming and Booth's Theatre went into bankruptcy. "I have done great things," Booth wrote a friend. "If you doubt me ask my creditors" (Kimmel 280). Booth's Theatre had company. Along with hundreds of other small-town theatres, the Grand Opera House also folded during the Panic. The New York City bank that held its mortgage foreclosed and it was sold to outside interests. Meanwhile, the loss of his beloved theatre condemned Booth to a life—albeit a financially lucrative one as the American theatre's greatest star—of wandering "from city to city, exhibiting his art in the midst of a system which was dying all around him" (Shattuck xxv). As the century wore on, Booth failed to keep up with new innovations in theatre—the ensemble company, the new native American drama, the new naturalistic acting styles that made his own work, once considered "naturalistic," seemed stilted and full of artifice. Fifteen years later, in the twilight of his brilliant career, Booth returned to Terre Haute with Lawrence Barrett (1838-91). They performed *Othello* on April 26, 1888 with Barrett in the title role and Booth as Iago. Barrett, at least in the eyes of Terre Hauteans, had eclipsed Booth's star by 1888. The local papers couldn't get enough of him—his temper tantrums, his private railroad car, his demands for a bigger share of ticket sales, and his arguments with the manager of the local theatre. It was reported that, angry at seeing Booth's portrait placed above his on a wall in the lobby of the Terre Haute House, Barrett flipped the photograph over, turning Booth's face to the wall. Little newspaper mention was made of Booth's activities, nothing was said of his 1873 appearance. Within five years he was dead.

But in 1873, at the age of 39, he was in full possession of the greatest dramatic powers ever witnessed in America. He appeared in numerous towns that season for one-night stands and coped with a faulty company, personal tragedies, and rude and boisterous audiences in an effort to bring his art to the Midwest and pay off his financial indebtedness. The citizens of Terre Haute, proud of their new Grand Opera House and hurt by the word "provincial" when applied to them, understood the historical and artistic importance of their distinguished theatrical visitor. The mixed civic pride they exhibited at his visit offers some interesting insights into the emerging cultural consciousness of the nineteenth-century Midwest.

Part Four

The Circus

Chapter 9
"Larceny in His Soul":
The Circus Grifter

No professional historian has written a definitive history of the American circus. At first glance this seems a curious omission given the considerable influence of the circus on American material and popular culture. But traditional modes of scholarship—the objective discovery, collection, verification, interpretation, criticism, and publication of pertinent evidence—aren't always useful when confronted with the sprawling, complex and mysterious subculture that constitutes the American circus. The major obstacle in producing a scholarly, comprehensive treatment is that, to a degree greater than any other American popular entertainment form, circus artifacts and historical evidence belong to "fans" rather than to traditional academic depositories such as university libraries and heavily-endowed private and public museums and institutions. Several of the largest and most significant collections consist of personal memorabilia still in private hands, and "the most knowledgeable students of circus history...remain the dedicated amateurs" (Flint 616). Lacking a professional historian's objectivity, published circus histories are notable for their selectivity and for their authors' own personal interests. As a result, "most of the literature dealing with the circus has dealt with its performers and owners" (Truzzi 183). Unimpeded by serious scholarly inquiry, the circus's past has been mythologized, elevated to almost hagiographical status, and eager tourists today flock to sites where enshrinement has occurred. Well-managed historical exhibits, such as the Circus World Museum at Baraboo, Wisconsin, and the winter quarters of Ringling Bros., Barnum & Bailey at Sarasota, Florida, perpetuate wistful images of graceful performers and the aroma of sawdust and cotton candy.

These exhibits, however, omit a rather unsavory element of the American circus, an element generally ignored because it doesn't quite square with the fascination and lure of the romantic elements of this perhaps greatest of all American popular entertainments. The plain, unvarnished truth is that during the nineteenth and early twentieth centuries many circuses and their side shows were thoroughly crooked and infested with grift, a term that designates dishonest circus practices requiring personal contact between criminal and victim. This illegal circus activity is a sensitive area usually swept under a collective rug. If it is mentioned at all, each circus generation conveniently blames an earlier generation for dishonesty. Sociologist Edwin H. Sutherland, whose work we will discuss in a moment, studied circus grift in the late 1930s and grew increasingly frustrated at this selective memory process.

The books on the circus which have been published since 1920 generally explain that there is no grifting in the circus at present but that practically all of the circuses around 1900 had grifting. The books written around 1900 explain that there was little grifting at that time, but there had been much grifting about 1880. And at least one book written in 1882 made the same contention regarding the superiority of that decade to the earlier decades...Most of the books on the circus have been written by managers, press agents, or performers in the circus and none of them are willing to admit that those of his own date are dishonest. (Sutherland)[1]

Sutherland was right. Early works on the circus such *The Ways of the Circus; Being the Memoirs of George Conklin, Tamer of Lions* (1921), John J. Jennings's *Theatrical and Circus Life* (1882), Robert Edmund Sherwood's *Here We Are Again: Recollections of an Old Circus Clown* (1926), Earl Chapin May's *The Circus from Rome to Ringling* (1932), and Bert J. Chipman's *Hey Rube* (1933) discuss grift, some even going so far as to suggest that it was a necessary evil for keeping "real" criminals out of the circus. But from the 1940s on, a sudden cultural amnesia occurs. What was once a parasitic, but vibrant and essential part of circus subculture, is treated as if it never existed. Recent books such as Myron Matlaw's anthology *American Popular Entertainment* (1979), David Lewis Hammarstrom's *Behind the Big Top* (1980), and John Culhane's *The American Circus: An Illustrated History* (1990) don't mention grift at all. George L. Chindahl's useful *A History of The Circus in America* (1959), unfinished and unindexed at the author's death, devotes a mere two sentences to grift. Circus grift in the last half of the twentieth century has received a polite and almost complete burial.

The remainder of this essay examines the phenomenon of grift and grifters in the American circus. It relies on three sources: (1) The unpublished field notes dating from the late 1930s of Edwin Hardin Sutherland (1893-1950), considered the founder of modern American criminology studies and coiner of the term "white collar crime;" (2) The unpublished autobiography and notes of one of Sutherland's informants, grifter Glenn H. Wakefield, alias "Ham Bannister" (1873-1938?); and (3) Tape recorded interviews and statements collected in the early 1980s by my colleague Professor Nels G. Juleus and me with circus actors and grifters who retired from the American circus before World War II. Most of these informants have since died.

Many circus lots at the turn of the twentieth century—98 shows were on the road in 1903—swarmed with sanctioned criminal activity. Sutherland, studying the phenomenon in 1938, found the circus "generally dishonest" during this period, describing it as a system that not only frequently withheld pay from its employees, but, along with legitimate circus acts and side show performers and in the age of "humbug" ushered in by P.T. Barnum, fooled its public with manufactured "natural" curiosities (geese eggs sold as "emu" eggs, for example), snake oil, and false advertising. Sutherland's evidence indicated that only two long-term successful circuses, Ringling Bros. Barnum & Bailey and Buffalo Bill's Wild West show, were totally free of grift, although strong evidence exists that others, such as the Hunt Bros. Circus and the Sparks Circus, may also have been "Sunday School," circus lingo for grift-free.[2]

Grift was an integral part of circus management for the simple reason that it was profitable and the criminal element extended throughout the circus hierarchy, starting at the top. Owners and managers, for example, actively encouraged their own employees, including actors, to gamble during off-duty hours in the "pie" or privilege car. The pie car was a railroad car usually leased from the circus by the "privilege" man, an individual paid by the circus owner or manager to regulate both the number of grifters and the kinds of grift and who tried "to get the best grifters he can, just like a university tries to get the best teachers it can" (Wakefield 31A). The pie car contained a short order restaurant, booths in which to eat and drink, and as many gaming devices as the rest of the space would hold. While these games were not rigged, odds were heavily in the house's favor. Consequently, a percentage of a gambling employee's salary reverted back to management. During the Great Depression, the manager of the Cole Bros. Circus reluctantly hired circus performers and workers on the strength of their reputation as heavy gamblers. An informant remembered how he operated.

He called over in Illinois and he was checking these guys: "Do they gamble?" If no, scratch them off the list. If they did, they at least got considered...The first month...the calliope player never did find his berth. He would play craps until they closed [the pie car] and crawled up on a crap table and get an hour or two sleep. Then they'd wake him up to play the calliope. (Informant #11)

Owners themselves weren't above direct involvement in illegal activities. The legendary Ben Wallace (1848-1921), owner of the Benjamin E. Wallace Circus, was accused of horse thievery, still a major crime at the turn of the century. A former Wallace employee described his technique.

I'll tell you how he got his horses. This fellow, we always called him Peedad. Wallace says, "Peedad, you see that team of bays over there?"
"Yessir."
"Get 'em."
"Yes sir."
Well, Peedad would hide around the wagon or lay in the wagon until the farmer climbed on the wagon and took them horses home. Peedad then would wait until he went to bed and he'd bring the horses back to the circus and then the circus would leave town. I'll tell you, in the old days the circus had an awful lot of conniving' goin' on. (Informant #6)

In fairness to Wallace it should be added that "he had the best stock in the market, and he knew how to treat horses. Nobody ever abused horses around his show" ("Circus Grift by An Old Circus Grifter" 3), even if they didn't belong to him. Some owners resisted grift, concentrating on presenting only acts and sideshows. W.C. Coup, sometime partner of P. T. Barnum, once squared off with a pair of six-shooters against a murderous grifter. Calling grifters that "blackleg fraternity," Coup later wrote, "My life has been frequently threatened and twice attempted because of my persistent determination to drive this thieving fraternity from my shows" (Coup 56).

A patron could be swindled on a grifting circus lot anywhere from the time he entered until the time he left; a dizzying array of illegal practices were possible. Some now seem humorous, but they probably weren't to the victims. Balloon men, for instance, were said to hire two accomplices ("boosters") who would walk through crowds puncturing children's balloon with a tack held between the teeth, a difficult feat under the best of circumstances. Parents were then forced to buy a new balloon for the child. Patrons, in a truly Barnumesque humbug, paid to enter a tent labeled "for men only" to discover a pair of suspenders hanging in mid-air instead of the striptease artists they anticipated.

Three types of grift, however, dominated: sure-fire gambling (also known as "flat-joint"), short changing, and picking pockets. Grifting circuses carried an inconspicuous "G-top" (gambling tent), and inside simple and fast gambling games and devices like three-card monte, cologne joints (so-named for the cheap colored cologne bottles used to lure customers), and shapes-and-miss-outs were the most popular. The faster the game, the bigger the turnover in money. A victim (called a "mark" or "sucker") could lose tens of dollars in a few minutes without being aware of it and grifters cannily watched for any signs of trouble. A man who worked from 1920 to 1935 for Hagenbeck-Wallace, Miller 101 Shows, and Sparks, commented,

Maybe the G-top would only be open three or four hours and they could score three or four or five thousand dollars. I've seen them take as much as $2,500 off one man. You know damn well they was gonna have a squawk. Well, if they took a big score like that, the gamblers would disappear and the top would come down. The sucker'd come back with the police: "Where's the gambling? Where?" No sign of anything. It's gone because they'd have that top down in five minutes and packed away. (Informant #13)

These games were all rigged. Absolutely no chance of winning existed unless a grifter wanted someone to win. For instance, a sucker could never find the pea in a shell game because the pea was never there. Made of the soft India rubber used for architect erasers and painted green, the pea was squeezed between the thumb and forefinger of the shell man ("Circus Grift by An Old Grifter" 38).

A second major grift, short changing, took place anywhere on the lot where money passed between patron and employee. Grifters working this operation included ticket sellers, popcorn sellers, candy butchers (who sold either candy or soft drinks), and balloon men. Here's an example of one kind of silver coin shortchanging called "crimp." A candy butcher tells a sucker he needs some larger change, perhaps half or silver dollars. For this favor to the butcher, the sucker is promised a free cup of pink lemonade, a truly awful concoction usually made of tartaric acid, saccharin, and a pinch of food coloring. Let's say the sucker gives the butcher two silver dollars. The butcher gives the man in return $1.90 in change and makes him count it. When the sucker discovers the dime shortage, the butcher takes the money back, the two count it together and the butcher admits his error. He adds a dime to the change, gives the money back to the sucker with one hand, while simultaneously handing him an overfilled cup of lemonade with the other hand. When the sucker tries to juggle the lemonade without spilling it, the butcher calmly palms all the quarters. The sucker usually ended up with $1 in dimes, nickels and pennies for his original two dollars. A good short changer reportedly could make as much as $100 to $150 a day using this technique ("Circus Grift by An Old Circus Grifter" 9-9A).

Candy butchers, however, were not allowed to short change paper money. That grift, called "slide," was the exclusive province of the ticket sellers, most of whom received no salary and whose livelihood depended entirely on what they could steal. Ticket selling perhaps was the easiest grift of all. The ticket box was often set up higher than a patron's eye level. The seller never put the change directly into the patron's hand, but spread out the correct change on a high mantle "beyond the reach of one swipe of the hand" so the patron couldn't reach all the paper or coins. If the patron later discovered the short change and returned, the seller would return the money and excuse himself by saying that he tried to get the buyer's attention but that he or she had already left (Letter, Parkinson to Zolbrod 5).

The third major grift on the circus lot was picking pockets. A male pickpocket was a "gun," a female a "gun-moll." The following story can be found in numerous accounts. This one comes from an informant who, as a young boy in the late nineteenth century, worked as a G-top lookout.

Now, they always had a lot of pickpockets around, you know. Well, the equestrian director [ringmaster] would get up and say, "Ladies and gentlemen! We do not tolerate pickpockets. We don't want them around here. If we find them we turn them over to the sheriff. But I'll tell you what I want you to do. I want all you men, right now, to look and see if you got your wallet."

Well, one man would look here and another man would look back here, and it showed the pickpockets right where the pocketbook is. Then it was time for them to get busy. This one had a long fish pole with a pin on the end of it. Just as the lion act would come in—everybody's always interested in the lion act— he'd get under the seats, see a man's pocketbook, you know, the big ones with the strings that stick out? He'd get right under there and lift it [with the fishing pole]. (Informant #6)[3]

Grifters and thieves operated with impunity because of interaction and cooperation among three elements: circus owners and managers, corrupt public officials, and victims. While "privilege men" managed grift on the lot, owners kept as much as forty per cent of everything stolen during a day's business. It's impossible to know just how much was stolen, but manager Will Irwin in 1909 estimated that shows earned eighty percent of their profits from grift (Irwin 83-83; qtd. Inciardi 593). Yankee Robinson's (1818-1884) circus, one of the nineteenth-century's most successful operations, also used grift for a majority of its profit (Sherwood 23). W.C. Coup commented "It is a lamentable fact that not a few of the wealthiest showmen in the country have swelled their fortunes by the 'rake-off' from the despicable gain of these blacklegs and tricksters" (Coup 58).

Owners and managers often rose from the ranks of the grifting criminal subculture, and several, contradicting Glenn Wakefield's proposition that "once a circus grifter, always one," went on to run "Sunday School" operations ("Notes"). Grifters who became top executives included John V. "Pogey" O'Brien (1836-1889), who once had four shows on the road simultaneously and who hoodwinked P.T. Barnum by leasing one of Barnum's shows and turning it into a grifting operation; Jeremiah Joseph "Jerry" Mugivan (1873-1930) of the American Circus Corporation; and J. Augustus Jones (d. 1918), a gambler and owner of the small two-car railroad Jones Bros. Shows. Jones told his advance man in 1915 that "If there's any gambling device I haven't got on my circus, it's because I haven't heard of it" (Informant

#15). And grift also flourished because circus owners not only wanted it, but employed the necessary muscle to keep it under control. According to one of his employees, Jerry Mugivan could,

> Just look at the crowd and take a look at the way they're dressed and he can come up with what he thinks you stole that day. And if he doesn't get his fair share, he would tell you about it. They called him "Turk" or "The Big Turk," and he had one of these habits, sort of, when you stepped out of line, he'd hit you. Everybody kicked back to the show. (Informant #11)

Wakefield, who was at one time Mugivan's partner, was sure that "if you cut him open, ice water would run out. Jerry had hard, bad eyes. Guys would tremble when he looked at them" (Wakefield, "Biographical Notes"). These owners and managers were tough, shrewd and without scruple. According to Wakefield,

> The manager of a circus is hard because the business makes him or else because it selects hard men. Everyone tries to beat the circus—business men, claimants of injuries, etc.,—just like they try to beat any big corporation. [These things] tend to make a manager hard...(1) Travel, rush, and pressure. (2) lack of physical conveniences while on the road. (3) The nut or overhead expense. (4) tough characters. You don't see nice people around a circus. (5) Strangers. People whom the circus manager has never seen before and will never see again. If he goes into the job of managing a circus a gentleman he will come out as a hard guy. (Wakefield "Circus—General")

Criminal activity on a circus lot also required dishonest public officials. Grifting circuses carried a "patcher" or "fixer" who insured through bribery that local police, district attorneys and other public officials didn't interfere with illegal practices. The fixer, who normally received ten to 15 percent of the net grift but no salary, usually had but one morning in which to size up local officials and determine what games would or would not be allowed on the circus lot. The fixer often lessened his impact as a community outsider by ingratiating himself with local politicians and joining several national fraternal organizations. Wakefield noticed that "A good fixer belongs to lots of clubs like Elks, Masons, Odd Fellows, Red Men. I've seen some of them with more pins on than Napoleon Bonaparte" ("Circus Grift by Circus Grifter"). To work without the protection of local authorities was hazardous. Here's an equestrian performer on, once again, Jerry Mugivan.

Anybody, ticket sellers or whoever, when you steal money [without police protection] you square your own beefs. If somebody nails you, you square it right now, whatever it costs, whatever you gotta do, you square it. If it doesn't get squared and it comes back to Mr. Mugivan, he comes and pays you off real fast. That's the end of you. You're gone. (Informant #2)

The third ingredient in grifting was the victim. It is no coincidence that the phrase "There's a sucker born every minute" is attributed to America's most famous circus owner. "There has never been," Sutherland lamented, "a scarcity of victims" ("Circus Grift" 4). The grifter, who considered himself a businessman and not a thief, actually thought little of the victim. "Grifters don't despise suckers." Wakerfield wrote. "They just don't pay any attention to them. Grifters think it is all right to trim a mark when they have paid protection for it...A grifter thinks that a man that gambles at another man's game *should* lose his money." The victim's stupidity was taken for granted. "Nobody reached in his pocket and robbed him," a former candy butcher noted. "He went into his own pocket and brought the money out" (Informant #13). The victim, displaying a common human trait, couldn't resist the chance to win something for nothing. But victims and other segments of the general public weren't wholly innocent in this chain of deceit. As Wakefield noted, public officials charged extortionate license fees, patrons might sneak into the circus grounds without paying, people brought unjustified injury and damage suits against owners, and elected officials demanded exorbitant numbers of free admission tickets. There was dishonesty on both sides.

What kind of man was the average grifter? Well, first of all he was just that—a man. Unlike the carnival, the circus had few women grifters. Exceptions included an occasional "mit reader" (fortune teller), gun-moll, or fish pond worker. During the 1880s, Dot Ailsworth earned a reputation as the "queen" of grifters by developing the simple, but effective fish pond game. Two dozen or so wooden fish (plastic ducks in the modern carnival version) had numbers printed on their bottoms to correspond to numbered prizes visible in the booth. The fish floated in a circular galvanized tank, only one-third of which was visible because a heavy curtain was drawn across it. Dot hired boosters to crouch behind the curtain and remove fish with winning numbers as they floated by (Ailsworth, "Biographical Notes").

Grifters normally used aliases or went by nicknames as colorful as their owners: Kid Cotton, Joe Frogg, The Leatherhead Kid, Jimmy Dallas, Overcoat Kelly, The Up and Down Kid, Red Brew, Knobby Clark, The Indiana Wonder. He usually launched his career with a short, but intensive, apprenticeship with a veteran forger or con man. A pickpocket, street gambler or candy butcher mentor was also highly prized by beginners because these grifts developed one's manual dexterity, sleight-of-hand, a rapid-fire patter, and the appearance of a non-aggressive, charming personality so necessary for circus gambling games. While many came from urban families with criminal backgrounds, most apparently were products of small-town America. Glenn Wakefield, for example, was born on a farm near Council Bluffs, Iowa, ran away from home at sixteen, and apprenticed with Jerry Mugivan, who called Terre Haute, Indiana, home, at the 1893 Chicago World's Fair (Sutherland, "Notes—Personal").

If skillful and lucky, the grifter worked his way up to flat-joints and G-tops, the elite of circus grift and a closed fraternity of professional thieves. The criminal nature of this mobile subculture and its notions of "otherness" from patrons, performers, and workers meant that deep attachments were formed. Grifters relied on their fraternity for security and familiarity, and once a grifter became attached to a particular circus, it was psychologically difficult to form an allegiance with another show. Wakefield described Archie Fenton, who, homesick for his old circus, Hagenbeck-Wallace, went back there and spent all his time and money drinking wine in the pie car instead of grifting. "Many other circus grifters are like that." he said. "A particular circus is their home and they can't feel right anywhere else. And he [Fenton] had been with the circus from a kid up" (Fenton, "Biographical Notes").

In 1936, Wakefield, in a "how-to" treatise, outlined the personal qualities necessary for successful grifting.

There are certain characteristics that a newcomer must have if he is to get along:

(1) he must have nerve and gall. Gall is fresh, impudence, while nerve is

courage and coolness under fire.
(2) he must be a good judge of human nature.
(3) he must read: newspaper, history, geography, philosophy.
(4) he must be able to think fast.
(5) he must have a good lookout.
(6) he must have good grift sense.
(7) he must have larceny in his soul.

These are much the same as the characteristics of a good salesman. A salesman can keep going even if he is not very successful, but a grifter goes to the penitentiary if he is not very successful. There is a more severe test on the grifter than on the salesman and for that reason a more highly selective process. (Wakerfield, "Training for Grift")

A good grifter did indeed have larceny in his soul. Nothing stood in the way of fleecing a mark. Shell game expert Bunk Allen, who bankrolled a show with the famous outlaws Frank James and Cole Younger, was stringing along a mark, who was accompanied by his little daughter, by allowing him to win several consecutive modest bets. When the girl wanted to go home and began crying, Allen, a billiard cue raised high above his head, charged around the table toward the poor girl and yelled, "Stop that whining, kid! Your father is winning!" Allen was too crooked even for a notorious bandit like Frank James, who reportedly withdrew from the show rather than associate with him (Allen, "Biographical Notes").

While other circus workers returned at the end of a season to a winter headquarters to rehearse acts, repair and paint equipment and train menageries and livestock, the successful grifter spent the winters basking in the sunshine of places like Hot Springs, Arkansas, a gambling center and a favorite gathering place for criminals before the advent of Las Vegas and Atlantic City, where they "had a good time losing all the jack they stole all summer." Many grifters teamed up with non-circus criminals and spent their off season wherever large amounts of money existed to be separated from marks— passenger trains, ocean liners, hotels, resorts, and race tracks. Still others "just stay home and loaf, or help the wife" ("Circus Grift by An Old Circus Grifter" 34). For all his native shrewdness and roguish personality, the grifter seldom had any luck at legitimate gambling himself and he usually began each circus season dead broke.

The grifter was looked down upon by circus actors, even though he lived better and made more money than performers. After all, his contribution to a season's profits was greater than any wild animal trainer or clown. Though not officially on any payroll and considered by the circus a necessary nuisance, he sometimes ate in the section of the cookhouse reserved for the owner or manager, but he was absolutely forbidden to speak to any performer or actor. At least that was the official line. Young female performers, however, liked to date grifters because they always carried ready cash. Wearing "track suits," girls would clandestinely meet grifters after the show by the railroad sidings where the circus train was parked (Informant #9).

Despite police protection on the lot, the life of a grifter was dangerous and several met violent deaths. E.M. Ballard, millionaire gambler and partner in the American Circus Corporation, was shot to death in Hot Springs in 1936. Soapy Smith was killed by a vigilante mob led by Iron Foot Johnson in Skagway, Alaska. Jerry Daley, who ran the pie car on the John Robinson Circus, was murdered by Cuban Frank in a Havana gambling house. The Up and Down Kid went down for good, murdered, in a pie car in Tripoli, Mississippi. Joe McCan, reputedly the greatest shell man who ever lived, was killed by a Wichita, Kansas, sheriff he had double-crossed in a scam ("Biographical Notes").

Circus grift declined steeply during the Great Depression and by 1946 it was virtually gone. The reasons for its disappearance are complex, but the primary reason was that it ceased being profitable. Circuses frequently changed names from season to season to avoid identification with grift, but by the late 1920s many operations found their name too popular and financially rewarding to risk changing. Hollywood cowboy stars like Tom Mix, Hoot Gibson, Ken Maynard, and Buck Jones (remember Frank James's experience with Bunk Allen?) sold their names and talents to the circus and most refused to appear with any grifting shows that would ruin their reputation with film audiences. Wakefield lamented in 1937,

The principle reason why the circuses have quit grifting is because it hurts business and causes a lot of trouble. A show doesn't like to be written up in the papers and the big shows can't afford to change their names if they get a bad reputation...All the big shows now bar grifting and are *square*...Some of the small shows are on the level now, too, but not all. (Circus Grift by an Old Circus Grifter 41)

In 1929, the Ringling corporation, an organization that had always been "Sunday School," bought out most of the larger grifting circuses for $2 million cash. Along with 150 railroad cars, 2,000 animals and 4,500 employees, it acquired an impressive list of show titles: Al G. Barnes, Hagenbeck-Wallace, John Robinson, Sells-Floto, Sparks, Buffalo Bill's Wild West Show, Howe's Great London. Now the largest and most influential circus organization ever and a "Sunday School" operation, Ringling Bros., Barnum & Bailey emphasized the circus as family entertainment (Culhane 220).

Grift died out, not because of any sudden moral change in circus management or in the American public, but simply because its adverse effects on public relations and the corporate aims of the Ringling group rendered it unprofitable. Pressed hard by alternative forms of entertainment in the modern age—" They don't need circuses now they got the movies," complained Wakefield—circuses consolidated, closed their railroad shows, and competed for a smaller share of the entertainment market (Sutherland, "Manuscript—Letters").

Where did the circus grifters go? They moved on to amusement parks, county fairs, and boardwalks like Atlantic City and Coney Island, where other grifters were already at work. A few lowered themselves to work in carnivals, a grift always considered the bottom rung of the professional ladder because it lacked genuine skill, brought in little cash and specialized in stealing money from children ("Circus—General"). But eventually most of these venues were closed, too, as large corporations, mindful of *their* public image and forming huge entertainment centers, promoted their holdings as wholesome family entertainment. The new entertainment and amusement park conglomerates, says popular theatre historian Don B. Wilmeth, are "packaging at its most persuasive best and an amazing example of organization know-how. Yet such concerns are no longer the products of professional showmen but the brainstorms of large corporations and businessmen" (Wilmeth vii). Marriott's Great America, Six Flags Over Texas, Disneyworld, and the new Ringling Bros. and Barnum & Bailey Combined Shows, Inc. have no place for the likes of Overcoat Kelly or The Up and down Kid. The old grifters died out, the younger ones lost their circus training grounds, and the remnants today, complained an old grifter to sociologists James A. Inciardi and David M. Peterson, are "just a bunch of young and clumsy catchpenny hustlers" (Inciardi and Peterson 601).

The disappearance of the circus grifter roughly paralleled the general demise of the itinerant popular entertainer in America. Shifting popular tastes and competition from new forms of mass entertainment robbed performers of their venues and, eventually, of their way of life. The panorama show, that marvelous expression of the Victorian values of self-education, intense interest in geography and organization "of the unfamiliar through picturization" (Hazelton 16), was swallowed up by the motion picture. Vaudeville and its stepchild burlesque took variety actors and minstrel shows off the road and packaged them for syndicated tours to medium-sized and large cities; these forms were in turn eclipsed by the motion picture and television. The modern museum movement created staid cultural institutions (imagine a natural history museum today advertising that it's "THOROUGHLY VENTILATED. Cool! Delightful!! Cool!!!") that upheld a new philosophy of what constitutes self-education. It was a philosophy that necessarily excluded the Feegee Mermaid and Sophia Ganz the Dwarf. A few wandering acts survived past mid-century, including small circuses with their occasional freak shows, small touring stock companies, family tent shows featuring "Toby," a freckle-faced, carrot-topped hayseed who was a favorite of rural audiences, and the ubiquitous medicine show.[8] The medicine show, with variety performers who sang, danced, performed plays and, reminiscent of the circus grifter, offered customers products too good to be true, hung on the longest, finally vanishing in the mid-1960s.[4]

It is true that the individuals in this book once enjoyed a measure of fame, that they experienced success, however short-lived, in the world of popular entertainment. It is also true that, with the possible exception of Edwin Booth, they are now obscure and forgotten. This should not diminish the importance of their professional lives. Their struggles and achievements offer us a richer view of popular culture in nineteenth-century America, scattered clues that form new textual evidence about the context of the live encounter between performer and audience. The experiences of William Henry Lane, the Bateman Sisters, John Banvard and the others are eloquent testimony to the diversity, vitality and tenacity of American popular entertainment before the coming of the age of electronic mass media. Long overlooked by scholars and serious writers, too often consigned to history's dustbin because their art was often ephemeral, peculiarly wedded to their age's popular taste or just plain bad by the standards of modern aesthetics, these people and their stories reinforce the view that human beings have a need to entertain and to be entertained, even if, in the case of the grifters, the entertained get hoodwinked in the bargain. "Audiences and my art are my reasons for living in this frail, uncertain world," wrote John Banvard, in a rare moment of self-reflection, when he was old, tired and deserted by his public. "But most of all, I wish to be remembered as an artist" (Banvard MS 6302). His words (laboriously written down on ragged leaves, as fragmentary as his life, torn from a ledger book) are self-conscious, commonplace—and utterly sincere. In the end, as it was with most of the rest of the people in this book, it didn't matter. "An actor's name," lamented the eighteenth-century tragedian David Garrick, "is writ on water."

Notes

Chapter One

[1]All events described and all quotations, unless otherwise noted, are from John Banvard's holograph autobiography (MS 6302, Banvard Family Papers .A219 [hereafter, BFP], Division of Archives and Manuscripts, Minnesota Historical Society, St. Paul, Minnesota). Banvard's autobiography consists of thirty-seven fragments, mostly torn from a ledger book, that describe his life from his New York City boyhood to his London 1848 panorama exhibition.

[2]Geneology Folder, BFP.

[3]Newspaper clipping, otherwise unidentified, Scrapbook; BFP.

[4]Unidentified folder, BFP.

[5]E[Edward]. T[Travers] Cox, unidentified newspaper clipping [*The Mortar?*], September 25, 1883, Library of the New Harmony Workingmen's Association; New Harmony, Indiana. Edward Travers Cox was employed by David Dale Owen as his assistant geologist. Fire eaters, both European and American, were a staple of nineteenth-century popular entertainments. See Ricky Jay, *Learned Pigs & Fireproof Women* (New York: Villard Books, 1986), [239]-273.

[6]Edith Banvard [John Banvard's daughter], "Notes," MS 4267, BFP.

Chapter Two

[1]Toll's bibliography (pp. 285-302) is the best compilation of sources on minstrelsy to date.

[2]The best study of the musical aspects of the minstrel show remains Hans Nathan's *Dan Emmett and the Rise of Early Negro Minstrelsy.*

[3]See *The Oxford Companion to the Theatre*, 3rd ed., Phyllis Hartnoll, ed., 645.

[4]Winter (28) claims the development of substituting dance for instrumental music was the result of the 1740 Slave Laws in which slaves were forbidden by plantation owners, fearful of the possiblity of an insurrection communicated by drum signals, to own or play musical instruments.

[5]Tom Bethune (1849-1908), "Black Tom," was a child prodigy who played the piano and appeared solo on stages throughout the South, and, after the Civil War, in the North. See Jay, [73]-[81].

[6]Handbill, Harvard Theatre Collection, Widener Library; Cambridge, Massachusetts.

[7]See Toll, *Blacking Up* 195-223; and Haskins, 34-53. Helen Armstead-

Johnson in her "Blacks in Vaudeville and Beyond" (Matlaw, pp. 77-86) examines the reactions of white managers, performers and stagehands to the presence of black entertainers.

Chapter Three

[1]Altick's work is supplemented by Ralph Hyde's *Panoramania! The Art and Entertainment of the "All-Embracing" View* (London: Trefoil Publications, 1988).

[2]Letter, Edith Banvard to Lawrence K. Fox, May 8, 1941, South Dakota Memorial Art Center; Daniel Boorstin, *The Americans: The National Experience* (New York: Random House, 1965), 238; Newspaper clipping, n.d., Scrapbook, BFP. The following scenes were listed in the 1847 Putnam Edition *Description*: Rush Island, Bluffs of Selma, Herculaneum, Plateen Rocks, Jefferson Barracks, Vide Pouche, United States Arsenal, St. Louis, Bloody Island, Missouri River, The Mouth of the Ohio, Cairo, Iron Banks, Chalk Banks, Mills Point, Indian Mounds, Plumb Point, Fulton, Randolph, Memphis, Fort Pickering, President's Island, Commerce, Stack Island, Vicksburg, Warrenton, Palmyra Island, Grand Gulf, Petite Gulf, Natchez, Ellis's Cliffs, Fort Adams, Bayou Sara, White Cliffs, Prophet's Island, Baton Rouge, Carrolton, La Fayette, New Orleans.

[3]Newspaper clipping, n.d., otherwise unidentified, Scrapbook, BFP; *Home Journal*, n.p., Feb., 12, 1848, Scrapbook, BFP.

[4]*Lynn Forum* (Massachusetts), July 24, 1847, Scrapbook, BFP.

[5]Newspaper clipping, n.d., otherwise unidentified, Scrapbook, BFP; Boorstin, 237; 239.

[6]Newspaper clipping, otherwise unidentified, annotated by Banvard, n.d., Scrapbook, BFP.

[7]Newspaper clipping, otherwise unidentified, Scrapbook, BFP; *New-York Times*, n.d., Scrapbook, BFP; *New-York Mercury*, n.d., Scrapbook, BFP.

[8]Newspaper clipping, n.d., otherwise unidentified, Scrapbook, BFP; *London Sun*, n.d., Scrapbook, BFP; Arrington, 232.

[9]Letter, Charles Dickens to John Banvard, December 16, 1848, BFP; John Banvard Dairy, n.d. [1848].

[10]McDermott, 162; Letter, Margery Tauber to author, February 7, 1979; newspaper clipping, n.d., Banvard Collection, South Dakota State Historical Society; Pierre, South Dakota.

[11]Newspaper clipping, n.d., otherwise unidentified, South Dakota Memorial Art Center; Records of Bureau of Marine Inspection and Navigation, National Archives, Washington, D.C.

Chapter Four

[1]New York Commerical Advertiser, March 1, 1852; Odell, III, 534. For a detailed account of some of the more prominent nineteenth century novelty acts,

see Jay, *Learned Pigs & Fireproof Women*. Laurence Hutton provides the title of this chapter in his discussion of "Infant Phenomena" in *Curosities of The American Stage* (New York: Harper and Brothers, 1891), 207-254.

[2]A modern acount of the Forrest-Macready feud can be found in Richard Moody's *The Astor Place Riot* (Bloomington: University of Indiana Press, 1958). The most accurate contemporary account is the anonymous pamphlet "Account of the Terrific and Fatal Riot at the New York Astor Place Opera House, on the Night of May 10th, 1849; With the quarrels of Forrest and Macready, Including All the Causes that Led to that Tragedy" (New York: H.N. Ranney, 1849).

Chapter Five

[1]Saxon, 89-112, provides the most complete account of the origins of Barnum's American Museum. A useful analysis of Barnum's publicity techniques may be found in John Dizikes, *Sportsmen and Gamesmen* (Boston: Houghton Mifflin, 1981).

[2]*The Mystery of San Marco* (USC #5616) was copyrighted May 25, 1876, and *Sun and Ice* (USC #3329) was copyrighted March 19, 1877. No copies were deposited in the Library of Congress. Library of Congress Copyright Office, *Dramatic Compositions Copyrighted in the United States: 1870-1916* (Washington, D.C., 1918), I, 1595; II. 2246.

[3]*New-York Times*, December 24, 1876; Odell, X, 217. *Corrinia* (USC #13767) was copyrighted on December 13, 1876 (*Dramatic Compositions*, I, 511), but Banvard may not have been the true author, plagiarizing or adapting Robert Buchanan's *Corinne* (USC #8515). See Patricia Marks, "Robert Buchanan's American Performances, 1876-95," *The Papers of the Bibliographical Society of America*, 74 (No. 2, 1980): 146-51.

Chapter Six

[1]Lee Simonson, *The Art of Scenic Design: A Pictorial Analysis of Stage Setting and its Relation to Theatre Production* (New York: Harper & Brothers, 1950), 34. Recent studies of the Saxe-Meiningen Court Theatre include: John Osbourne, *The Meininger Court Theatre* (Cambridge: Cambridge University Press, 1988); Steven DeHart, *The Meininger Theater: 1776-1926* (Ann Arbor, Michigan: UMI Research Press, 1981); Ann Marie Koller, translator, *Max Grube's The Story of the Meininger* (Coral Gables, Flordia: University of Miami Press, 1963).

[2] Milwaukee *Journal*, March 30, 1892. Ludwig Chronegk himself wasn't immune to actor revolts. Therese Grunert walked out in the middle of a Berlin performance of *The Winter's Tale* and sued the Court Theatre for refusing her a major role in another play. See DeHart, 41.

[3]The following is an alphabetical list of 43 German actors and actresses

who are known to have appeared as "The Meininger" during the 1891-1892 tour: Marianne Bedecovics, Julia Behr, Max Bleger, Ferdinand Brehm, Emil Brückmann, Willie Burke, Mathias Claudius, Margarethe Damm, Christian Eckelmann, Ehrich Gottlieb, Hans Graus, Emma Greibe, Therese Gutfield, Fritz Hamboecker, Moritz Haskh, Anna Haverland, Emil Hock, Willie Klein, Gustav Kober, Hilmar Knorr, George Lebret, Adolph Lenau, Hedwig Lilia, Otto Lindner, Carl Machold, V. Müller-Fabricus, Richard Oeser, Oscar Pelz, Mathieu Pfeil, Carl Rhomius, Gustav Rickelt, Henreich Rupprecht, Max Sieger, Carl Sick, Helene Strassmann, Julius Strassmann, Franz Richy, Carl Walles, Joseph Weber, Bernard Weinkaus, Karl Weiser, Marie Werner, and Jacob Wirth.

Chapter Seven

[1]McDermott underestimates the number of different plays presented by these companies. See Arthur W. Bloom's test of McDermott's thesis in his "The Jefferson Company, 1830-1845," *Theatre Survey* 12 (May/November 1986): 89-153. For accounts of phase one and two companies in Indiana, see Chapter I; Samuel L. Weinfeld, "A Survey of Early Theatrical Activity at New Harmony, Indiana," master's thesis, Indiana University, 1964; and Eva Draegert, "The Theatre in Indianapolis Before 1880," *Indiana Magazine of History* 51 (June 1955): 121-38. The most complete record of phase three companies in larger Ohio Valley cities is Weldon B. Durham, ed., *American Theatre Companies, 1749-1887*, vol. 1 (Westport, Connecticut: Greenwood Press, 1986).

[2]Grimsted, 49. The first solid evidence of a community-wide amateur performance is a January 24, 1862, German Theatrical Society benefit for German-born Civil War volunteers. *Wabash Express* January 24, 1862. This is an unlikely late date; in its early years Terre Haute, like many frontier settlements, had a flourishing literary society which read and probably produced dramas.

[3]The relationship between Miss Julia Blake, Julia Weston Blake, and Orlando Blake isn't known. Both women were in the same cast list for one production, so, unless Julia Weston Blake played two different roles, a not uncommon occurrence in small companies, these are two different individuals.

[4]Following is a list of the 114 plays produced during the 1857-58 season. Titles have been standardized according to Allardyce Nicoll's Hand-List in *A History of English Drama 1660-1900*, 2nd ed., vols. 3-6 (Cambridge: Cambridge University Press, 1963) and Donald Mullen's *Victorian Plays: A Record of Significant Productions on the London Stage, 1837-1901* (Westport, Connecticut: Greenwood Press), 1987. *Alarming Sacrifice/ An Object Of Interest/ The Bull in a China Shop/ The Bould Soger Boy/ The Cabin Boy/ Camille, or, The Fate of a Coquette/ Carline, The Female Brigand/ Charles II; or, The Merry Monarch/ Christine of Poland/ Damon and Pythias/ Delicate*

Ground; or, Paris in 1793/ Diamond; or, Buttons all Over Me/ Don Caesar De Bazan/ The Drunkard; or, The Fallen Saved/ Dumb Belle/ Eton Boy/ Factory Girl; or, All That Glitters Is Not Gold/ Faint Heart Never Won Fair Lady/ Family Jars/ Fazio, or, The Italian Wife/ The Forest Rose, or, The American Farmer/ The Freemason/ Ginger Blue/ Glance At New York/ Golden Farmer/ The Good For Nothing/ The Idiot Witness; or, A Tale Of Blood/ Honest Thieves/ The Honey Moon/ The Hunchback/ In And Out of Place/ Ingomar The Barbarian/ Ireland As It Is/ Irish Assurance And Yankee Modesty/ Irish Emigrant; or, Temptation?/ Irish Nighingales/ Irish Tiger/ Irish Tutor; or, New Lights/ Jack Sheppard and Joe Blueskin; or, Amateur Road Agents/ A Kiss In The Dark/ Lady Of The Lions; or Clod, The Bellows Mender/ The Lady Of Lyons; or, Love And Pride/ La Tour De Nesle, or, The Chamber of Death/ Landlords And Tenants, Or Paddy At Home/ Limerick Boy/ The Loan Of A Lover/ Lottery Ticket; or, The Lawer's Clerk/ Lucretia Borgia/ Macbeth, Act IV and V/ The Maid Of Croissey; or, Theresa's Vow/ Maniac Lover/ Margaret Catchpole/ Marie; or, The Daughter of the Regiment/ The Miser's Daughter/ More Blunders Than One/ Mr. and Mrs. White/ Nature And Philosophy/ New York Firemen/ The Omnibus! or, A Convenient Distance!/ Our Gal/ Perfection; or, The Maid of Munster/ Pettibones/ Pleasant Neighbor/ Pocahontas/ Poor Pillicoddy/ Prairie Flower, or, The Hoosier Farmer/ The Rent Day/ Richard III/ Rob Roy /Robert Emmett/ Romeo And Juliet/ Rosina Meadows; or, Temptation Unveiled/ Rough Diamond; or, Buttons All Over Me/ Sam Slick/ The Secret: or, A Hole In The Wall/ Six Degrees of Crime/ Sketches In India/ The Soldier's Return; or, What Can Beauty Do?/ Sophia's Supper, or The Robbers Of The Heath/ The Spectre Bridegroom; or, A Ghost In Spite Of Himself/ A Stage-Struck Barber/ State Secrets; or, The Tailor Of Tamworth/ The Stranger/ The Swiss Swains/ The Taming Of The Shrew/ Teddy Roe/ Terre Haute Firemen/ That Boy Jake/ Theresa; or, The Orphan Of Geneva/ The Thumping Legacy/ The Toodles/ The Two Gregories; or, Where Did The Money Come From?/ Uncle Tom's Cabin/ The Virginia Mummy/ Who Speaks First?/ Wife For A Day/ William Tell/ Woman; or, The Momentous Question/ The Yankee Clock Peddler/ Yankee Doorkeeper/ Yankee Duelist/ Yankee Ticket Taker/ The Young Widow; or, A Lesson For Lovers.

⁵*Daily Union*, October 3, 1858; November 23, 1858. For accounts of Terre Haute theatres in the later nineteenth century, see Marlene Kalbfleisch, "The Terre Haute Grand Opera House, 1869-1874," master's thesis, Indiana State University 1972 and Mary Elena Giglio, "The Terre Haute Grand Opera House, 1897-1898," master's thesis, Indiana State University, 1974.

⁶*Daily Union*, April 18, 1858; Odell, VI, 460; Odell, VI, 648; VIII 23; Durham, "California Theatre Stock Company," in Durham, 51; John M. Callahan, "DeBar's Grand Opera House Stock Company," in Durham, 250; John S. Kendall, *The Golden Age of the New Orleans Theatre* (Baton Rouge:

Louisiana State University Press, 1952), 406; Ludlow, 304; Samuel L. Leiter, "Park Theatre Company," in Durham, 415; J.P. Wearing, *American and British Theatrical Biography: A Directory* (Metuchen: The Scarecrow Press, 1979), 857.

[7]Francis Hodge, in his introduction to the reprint of Ludlow's *Dramatic Life As I Found It*, notes that the region was "tamed by a rough stock of hardy individuals who drank whiskey, spit precariously...[and] consumed enormous meals of beefsteak (v, vi). Terre Hauteans, proud of their civic accomplishments, however modest, by 1858 would have greeted this characterization of their founders with great indignation, however truthful it may have been.

Chapter Eight

[1]A thorough history of the beginnings of the Grand Opera House is contained in Kalbfleisch, "The Terre Haute grand Opera House, 1969-1874."

[2]Owens became an overnight star when he appeared in the New York production of Sidney Cowell Bateman's *Self*. See Chapter 3.

Chapter Nine

[1]Professor Sutherland's notes on grifting were generously shared with the author by Donald Cressey, late of the University of California at Santa Barbara, a student of Sutherland's, and himself one of America's foremost sociologists of crime.

[2]Sutherland, "Circus Grift," EHSP, 1-4. Letter, Robert L. Parkinson (late curator of the Circus World Museum, Baraboo, Wisconsin) to Joan Zolbrod, August 12, 1982; Files, Allegheny College Public Information Office; Meadville, Pennsylvania. For an examination of humbug and the relationship of the American showman and his public, see John Dizikes's *Sportsman and Gamesmen*.

[3]A list of games can be found in J.C.R. MacDonald, *Crime is a Business: Buncos, Rackets, Confidence Games* (Stanford: Stanford University Press, 1938); and Edward H. Smith, "Invention and the Grifter, *Scientific American* 129 (August 1923), 78-79, 135, 142-43; "The Inventor and the Gay Gambler," *Scientific American* 129 (September 1923), 150-51, 215-16. Two influential studies of non-circus grift should be noted: Sutherland's own *The Professional Thief: a Professional Thief* (Chicago: The University of Chicago Press, 1937); and David W. Mauerer's *The Big Con: The Story of The Confidance Man and The Confidence Game* (Indianapolis: The Bobbs-Merrill Co., 1940).

[4]For studies of these forms, see Douglas Gilbert's *American Vaudeville* (New York: Dover Publications, Inc., 1963); Henry Holtman's *Freak Show Man* (Los Angeles: Halloway House, 1968); Harlowe R. Hoyt's *Town Hall Tonight* (New York: Bramhall House, 1955) [stock companies]; William

Lawrence Slout's *Theatre in a Tent* (Bowling Green, Ohio: Bowling Green University Popular Press, 1972) ["Toby" shows]; and Brooks McNamara's *Step Right Up* (New York: Doubleday & Company, Inc., 1976) [medicine shows].

Works Cited

I. Primary Sources

A. *Unpublished Materials*

Banvard Collection. South Dakota State Historical Society. Pierre, SD.

Banvard Family Papers .A219. Division of Archives and Manuscripts. Minnesota Historical Society, St. Paul, MN.

Banvard File. South Dakota Memorial Art Center. Brookings, SD.

Banvard File. Watertown Regional Library. Watertown, SD.

"Diary of Enoch Honeywell, April 1818," Unpublished Manuscript. Emeline Fairbanks Memorial Library. Terre Haute, IN.

Hahn, Henry. "Map of Terre Haute, Indiana, in 1864." Watercolor Map. Archives, Historical Museum of the Wabash Valley. Terre Haute, IN.

Informant #6. Wagon painter, G-top lookout; Wallace Combined Shows, Hagenbeck- Wallace, Cole Bros.-Clyde Beatty Circus, 1914-50. Tape Recorded Comments [1967?]. Re-recorded 12 June 1980. Peru, IN.

Informant #2. Interview. Equestrian act; Hagenbeck-Wallace, several other American and European circuses, 1925-52. 11 June 1980. Peru, IN.

Informant #9. Interview. General Useful [acrobat, elephant rider, miscellaneous acts]. American Circus Corporation, Al G. Barnes and Sells-Floto Combined Circuses, Cole Bros.-Clyde Beatty Circus, 1920-38. 13 June 1980. Peru, IN

Informant #11. Interview. Clown, Cole Bros.-Clyde Beatty Circus, 1930s. 12 June 1980, Peru, IN.

Informant #13. Interview. Candy butcher, bally act, side show sword swallower, mind-reading act; Hagenbeck-Wallace, Miller 101 Shows, and Sparks, 1920-37. 19 Aug. 1980; Erie, PA.

Informant #15. Interview. Publicist, advance man; Jones Bros. Circus, 1911-17. 27 Aug. 1980. Jamestown, NY.

Lilliendahl, William A. "Memoranda of Matters relative to John Banvard and the New York Museum Association." n.d. Holograph manuscript with annotations #3307. Manuscript Collections, New-York Historical Society. New York, NY.

"Minutes." 28 February 1835-12 July 1836. New Harmony Thespian Society. Library of the New Harmony Workingmen's Association. New Harmony, IN.

"Minutes of the City Council Meetings 1840-41." Terre Haute, Indiana. Archives, Historical Museum of the Wabash Valley. Terre Haute, IN.

"Old Wabash Valley Settlers Association Minutes of 1875." Typewritten. Emeline Fairbanks Memorial Library. Terre Haute, IN.

Robinson, Doane. "John Banvard." Typewritten [1939?]. South Dakota Memorial Art Center. Brookings, SD.

Sutherland, Edwin H. "Circus Grift." Typewritten manuscript. [1938?].

[Wakefield, Glenn H., "Ham Bannister]. "Biographical Notes." Typewritten. [1938?].

_____."Circus—General." Typewritten. [1938?].

_____."Circus Grift by An Old Circus Grifter." Typewritten Manuscript. [1938?].

_____."Training for Grift." Typewritten. [1938?]

B. Periodicals and Pamphlets

Account of the Terrific and Fatal Riot at the New York Astor Place Opera House, on the Night of May 10th, 1849; With the Quarrels of Forrest and Macready, Including All the Causes that Led to that Tragedy. New York: H.N. Ranney, 1849. *Athenaeum,* 1851.

[Banvard, John]. *Description of Banvard's Panorama of the Mississippi, Painted on Three Miles of Canvas, exhibiting a View of Country 1200 Miles in Length, Extending from the Mouth of the Missouri River to the City of New Orleans, Being by far the largest Picture ever executed by Man.* Boston: John Putnam, 1847.

[Banvard, John]. "John Banvard's Great Picture-Life on the Mississippi." *Littell's Living Age* 15 (December 1847): 509-516.

"Banvard's Panorama." *Scientific American* 4 (16 December 1848): 100.

Cox, E[Edward]. T[Travers]. Unidentified newspaper clipping [*The Mortar* (New Harmony, Indiana)?], 25 September 1883.

C. Newspapers

Boston *Journal,* 1847, 1864.

Boston Morning Advertiser, 1864.

Buffalo *Morning Express,* 23 October 1849.

Indianapolis *Journal,* 1870.

London Illustrated News, 1848; 1851.

Louisville *Morning Courier,* 1846.

Milwaukee *Daily Sentinel,* 1850.

Milwaukee *Journal,* 1892.

Milwaukee *Sentinel,* 1892.

New York *Commerical Advertiser,* 1852.

New York Daily Tribune, 1867.

New York *Herald*, 1849; 1852; 1892
New York *Sun*, 1891.
New-York Times, 1876, 1891.
St. Louis *Post-Dispatch*, 1892.
Terre Haute (Indiana) *Daily Express*, 1873.
Terre Haute (Indiana) *Daily Journal*, 1852; 1853
Terre Haute (Indiana) *Daily Union*, 1858; 1873.
Terre Haute (Indiana) *Evening Gazette*, 1873.
Terre Haute (Indiana) *Journal*, 1870.
Terre Haute (Indiana) *Saturday Evening Mail*, 1873.
Terre Haute (Indiana) *Wabash Courier*, 1841.
Terre Haute (Indiana) *Wabash Express*, 1852; 1861; 1862
Watertown (South Dakota) *Public Opinion*, 1891.
Western Register & Terre Haute Advertiser (Indiana), 1823.

D. Miscellaneous

Huntington (New York) Township Records. Suffolk County Historical Society. Riverhead, Long Island, New York.
Library of Congress Copyright Office. *Dramatic Compositions Copyrighted in the United States: 1870-1916*. Washington, D.C., 1918.
Terre Haute City Directory 1853.
Terre Haute City Directory 1858.
Terre Haute City Directory 1868-1869.

II. Secondary Sources
A. Books

Altick, Richard. *The Shows of London*. Cambridge, Massachusetts: Harvard UP, 1978.
Armstead-Johnson, Helen. "Blacks in Vaudeville and Beyond." *American Popular Entertainment*, Myron Matlaw, Editor. Westport, CT: Greenwood Publishers, 1979.
Barnes, Eric Wollencott. *The Lady of Fashion: The Life and the Theatre of Anna Cora Mowatt*. NY: Charles Scribner's Sons, 1954.
Boorstin, Daniel. *The Americans: The National Experience*. NY: Random House, 1965.
Bradsby, H.C. *History of Vigo County*. Chicago: Hill and Iddings, 1891.
Brown, T. [Thomas] Allston. *History of the American Stage, Containing Biographical Sketches of Nearly Every Member of the Profession that has Appeared on the American Stage from 1733 to 1870*. NY, 1870; reprint, NY Benjamin Blom, 1969.
_____. *A History of the New York Stage: From the First Performance in 1732 to 1901*. Three Volumes. NY: Dodd, Mead, and Company, 1903.

_____."The Origin of Minstrelsy." *Fun in Black, or, Sketches of Minstrel Life.* Charles H. Day, Editor. NY: R.M. DeWitt, 1874.

Buley, R. Carlyle. *The Old Northwest Period, 1815-1840.* Two Volumes. Indianapolis: IN Historical Society, 1950.

Carlson, Marvin. *The German Stage in the Nineteenth Century.* Metuchen, NJ: The Scarecrow P, 1972.

Carson, William G.B. *The Theatre on the Frontier: The Early Years of the St. Louis Stage.* Chicago: The U of Chicago P, 1932.

Coup, W[William]. C[Cameron]. *Sawdust and Spangles.* New York, 1901; reprint, Washington, D.C.: Paul A. Ruddell, 1961.

Courlander, Harold. *Negro Folk Music, USA.* NY: Columbia UP, 1963.

Cowell Joseph. *Thirty Years Passed Among the Players in England and America.* NY: Harper, 1844.

Csida, Joseph and Csida, June Bundy. *American Entertainment: A Unique History of Popular Show Business.* Watson-Guptill Publication, 1978.

Culhane, John. *The American Circus: An Illustrated History.* NY: Henry Holt and Company, 1991.

Daly, Joseph Francis. *The Life of Augustin Daly.* NY: Macmillan, 1917.

DeHart, Steven. *The Meininger Theater: 1776-1926.* Ann Arbor, MI: UMI Research P, 1981.

Dickens, Charles. *American Notes* in *The Works of Charles Dickens.* Volume 27. NY: Peter Fenton Collier, [1911?].

Dizikes, John. *Sportsmen and Gamesmen.* Boston: Houghton, Mifflin, 1981.

Dunlap, William. *History of the American Theatre.* Second Editon: Three Volumes in One. London, 1833; reprint, NY: Burt Franklin, 1963.

Durham, Weldon B. Editor. *American Theatre Companies, 1749-1887.* Three Volumes. Westport, CT: Greenwood P, 1986.

Engle, Gary D. *This Grotesque Essence: Plays from the American Minstrel Stage.* Baton Rouge: Louisiana State UP, 1978.

Felheim, Marvin. *The Theatre of Augustin Daly: An Account of the Late Ninteenth Century American Stage.* Cambridge: Harvard UP, 1956.

Ford, George D. *These Were Actors.* NY: Library Publishers, 1955.

Gernsheim, Helmut and Alison. *L.J.M. Daguere (1787-1851).* Cleveland: World Publishing Company, 1956.

Gilbert, Douglas. *Lost Chords: The Diverting Story of American Popular Songs.* Garden City, New York: Doubleday, Doran and Co., Inc., 1942.

_____. *American Vaudeville.* NY: Dover Publications, Inc., 1963.

Graham, Philip. *Showboats: The History of an American Institution.* Austin: U of Texas P, 1951.

Grimsted, David. *Melodrama Unveiled: American Theater and Culture 1800-1850.* Chicago: U of Chicago P, 1968.

Grossman, Edwina Booth. *Edwin Booth.* Reprint; Freeport, NY: Books for

Libraries P, 1970.

Harris, Neil. "Four Stages of Cultural Growth: The American City." *Indiana Historical Society Lectures, 1970-1972.* Indianapolis: Indiana Historical Society, 1972.

_____. *Humbug: the Art of P.T. Barnum.* Boston: Little, Brown and Company, 1973.

Haskins, James. *Black Theater in America.* NY: Thomas Y. Crowell, 1982.

Heaps, Williard and Porter W. *The Singing Sixties.* Norman: U of Oklahoma, 1960.

Hewitt, Bernard. *Theatre U.S.A.* NY: McGraw-Hill, 1959.

Holtman, Henry. *Freak Show Man.* Los Angeles: Halloway House, 1968.

Howard, John Tasker. *Our American Music.* NY: Thomas Y. Crowell, 1946.

Hoyt, Harlowe R. *Town Hall Tonight.* NY: Bramhall House, 1955.

Hutton, Laurence. *Curiosities of the American Stage.* NY: Harper and Brothers, 1891.

Jay, Ricky. *Learned Pigs & Fireproof Women.* NY: Villard Books, 1986.

Jefferson, Joesph. *The Autobiography of Joseph Jefferson.* NY: Century Company, 1890.

Jones, Bessie and Hawes Bess Lomax. *Step It Down: Games, Plays, Songs, and Stories from the Afro-American Heritage.* NY: Harper & Row, 1972.

Kendall, John S. *The Golden Age of the New Orleans Theatre.* Baton Rouge: Louisiana State UP, 1952.

Kimmel, Stanley. *The Mad Booths of Maryland,* Second Edition. NY: Dover Publications, Inc., 1969.

Knapp, Bettina and Chapman, Myra. *That Was Yvette: The Biography of Yvette Guilbert, The Great Diseuse.* NY: Holt, Rinehart, Winston, 1964.

Koller, Ann Marie, Translator. *Max Grube's The Story of the Meininger.* Coral Gables, FL: U of Miami P, 1963.

Kosch, Wilhelm. *Deutsches Theater-Lexicon.* Three Volumes. Klagenfurt, Austria: Verlay Ferd. Kleinmayr, 1953-71.

Leavitt, Michael B. *Fifty Years in Theatrical Management.* NY: Broadway Publishing Company, 1912.

Lockridge, Richard. *Darling of Misfortune.* NY: Century Co., 1932.

Longfellow, Henry Wadsworth. *Kavanaugh* in *Longfellow's Works.* Boston: Houghton, Mifflin, 1904.

Longfellow, Samuel. *Life of Henry Wadsworth Longfellow, With Extracts From His Journals and Correspondence.* Two Volumes. Boston: Ticknor and Company, 1886.

Ludlow, Noah M. *Dramatic Life As I Found It: A record of personal experience; with an account of the rise and progress of the drama in the West and South, with anecdotes and biographical sketches of the principal actors and actresses who have at times appeared upon the stage in the Mississippi*

Valley. St. Louis, 1880; reprint, NY: Benjamin Blom, 1966.

MacDonald, J.C.R. *Crime is a Business: Buncos, Rackets, Confidence Games.* Stanford: Stanford UP, 1938.

Maurer, David W. *The Big Con: The Story of the Confidence Man and the Confidence Game.* Indianapolis: The Bobbs-Merrill Co., 1940.

McDermott, John Francis. *The Lost Panoramas of the Mississippi.* Chicago: U of Chicago P, 1958.

McNamara, Brooks, Editor. *American Popular Entertainments.* New York: Performing Arts Journal Publications, 1983.

_____. *Step Right Up.* NY: Doubleday & Company, Inc., 1976.

Moody, Richard. *The Astor Place Riot.* Bloomington: U of Indiana P, 1958.

Moses, Montrose J. *Representative Plays by American Dramatists.* Three Volumes. NY: Little, Brown, and Company, 1918-25.

Mullen, Donald. *Victorian Plays: A Record of Significant Productions on the London Stage, 1837-1901.* Westport, CT: Greenwood P, 1987.

Nathan, Hans. *Dan Emmett and the Rise of Early Negro Minstrelsy.* Norman, OK: U of Oklahoma P, 1962.

Nicoll, Allardyce. *A History of English Drama 1660-1900.* Second Edition, Six Volumes. Cambridge: Cambridge UP, 1963.

Oakey, C.C. *Greater Terre Haute and Vigo County.* Two Volumes. Chicago: Lewis, 1908.

Odell, George C.D. *Annals of the New York Stage.* Fifteen Volumes. NY: Columbia UP, 1927-49.

Osbourne, John. *The Meininger Court Theatre.* Cambridge: Cambridge UP, 1988.

Rahill, Frank. *The World of Melodrama.* University Park: Pennsylvania State UP, 1967.

Robinson, Alice; Roberts, Vera Mowry; Barranger, Milly S., Editors. *Notable Women in the American Theatre,* Westport, CT: Greenwood P, 1989.

Roehm, Marjorie Catlin. *The Letters of George Catlin and His Family: A Chronicle of the American West.* Berekley: U of California P, 1966.

Ruggles, Eleanor. *The Prince of Players.* NY: W.W. Norton, 1953.

Sandburg, Carl. *Abraham Lincoln: The War Years.* Four Volumes. NY: Charles Scribner's Sons,1939.

Saxon, A.H. *P.T. Barnum: The Legend and the Man.* NY: Columbia UP, 1989.

Schick, Joseph S. *The Early Theatre in Eastern Iowa.* Chicago: U of Chicago P, 1939.

Shattuck, Charles H. *The Hamlet of Edwin Booth.* Urbana: U of Illinois P, 1969.

Sherwood, Robert Edmund. *Hold Yer Hosses, the Elephants are Coming.* NY: Macmillan, 1932.

Simonson, Lee. *The Art of Scenic Design: A Pictorial Analysis of Stage Setting and its Relation to Theatre Production.* NY: Harper & Brothers, 1950.

Slout, William Lawrence. *Theatre in a Tent*. Bowling Green, OH: Bowling Green State University Popular Press, 1972.

Smith, Solomon. *Theatrical Apprenticeship. comprising a sketch of the first seven years of his professional life; together with anecdotes and skeches of adventure in after years*. Philadelphia: T.B. Peterson, 1845.

Smither, Nellie. *A History of the English Theatre in New Orleans*. 1944; NY: Benjamin Blom, 1966.

Spann, Edward K. *The New Metropolis: New York City, 1840-1857*. NY: Columbia UP, 1981.

Stearns, Marshall and Jean. *Jazz Dance: The Story of American Vernacular Dance*. NY: The Macmillan Co., 1968.

Still, Bayrd. *Milwaukee: The History of a City*. Madison: The State Historical Society of Wisconsin, 1948.

Sutherland, Edwin H. *The Professional Thief: by a Professional Thief*. Chicago: The U of Chicago P, 1937.

Toll, Robert. *Blacking Up: The Minstrel Show in Nineteenth-Century America*. NY: Oxford UP, 1974.

_____. "Show Biz in Blackface: The Evolution of the Minstrel Show as a Theatrical Form." *American Popular Entertainment: Papers and Proceedings of the Conference on the History of American Popular Entertainment*. Myron Matlaw, Editor. Westport, CT: Greenwood P, 1977.

Toole-Stott, Raymond. *Circus and Allied Arts: A World Bibiiography, 1500-[1970]*, Four Volumes. Derby, England: Harpur, [1958-71].

Truzzi, Marcello. "Circus and Side Shows." *American Popular Entertainment*, Myron Matlaw, Editor. Westport, CT: Greenwood Publishers, 1979.

Wearing, J.P. *American and British Theatrical Biography: A Directory*. Metuchen, New Jersey: The Scarecrow Press, 1979.

Wemyss, Frederick Courtney. *Chronology of the American Stage, 1752-1852*. NY, 1852; reprint, NY: Benjamin Blom, 1968.

Wilmeth, Don B. *The Language of Popular Entertainment*. Westport CT: Greenwood P, 1981.

Wilson, William E. *Indiana: A History*. Bloomington: Indiana UP, 1966.

Wittke, Carl. *Tambo and Bones: A History of the American Minstrel Stage*. Durham, NC: Duke UP, 1930.

Wright, Richardson. *Hawkers and Walkers in Early America: Strolling Peddlers, Preachers, Lawyers, Doctors [sic] Players, and Others, from the Beginning to the Civil War*. Philadelphia: J.B. Lippincott, 1927.

B. Articles

Arrington, Joseph Earl. "John Banvard's Moving Panorama of the Mississippi, Missouri, and Ohio Rivers." *The Filson Club History Quarterly* 32 (July, 1958): 207-40.

Bloom, Arthur W. "The Jefferson Company, 1830-1845." *Theatre Survey* 12 (May/ Nov. 1986): 89-153.

Cohen, Richard. "Hamlet as Edwin Booth," *Theatre Survey* 10 (May 1969): 53-59.

Dondore, Dorothy Ann. "Banvard's Panorama and the Flowering of New England." *New England Quarterly* 11 (1938): 817-26.

Draegert, Eva. "The Theatre in Indianapolis Before 1880." *Indiana Magazine of History* 51 (June 1955): 121-38.

Flint, Richard W. "A Selected Guide to Source Material on the American Circus." *Journal of Popular Culture* 6 (Winter 1972): 615-618.

Hazelton, Nancy J. Doran. "The Tourist in the Audience: Travel Pictures on the Nineteenth-Century Stage." *Theatre History Studies* 12 (1992): 13-24.

Heilbron, Bertha L. "John Banvard's New York." *Antiques* 56 (August 1949): 108-09.

Inciardi, James A. and Peterson, David M. "Gaff Joints and Shell Games: A Century of Circus Grift." *Journal of Popular Culture* 6 (Winter 1972): 591-598.

Marks, Patricia. "Robert Buchanan's American Performances, 1876-95." *The Papers of the Bibliographical Society of America* 74 (No. 2, 1980): 146-51.

McDermott, Douglas. "The Development of the Theatre on the American Frontier, 1750-1890," *Theatre Survey* 19 (May 1978): 63-78.

Meersman, Roger. "The Meininger in America." *Speech Monographs* 33 (Mar., 1966): 40-49.

Newman, Estelle. "The Story of 'Banvard's Folly.' " *Long Island Forum* 11 (May 1952): 83-4; 95-7.

Robertson, John E.L. "Paducah: Origins to Second Class." *The Register of the Kentucky Historical Society* 66 (Apr., 1968): 108-36.

Roll, Charles. "Indiana's Part in the Nomination of Abraham Lincoln for President in 1860." *Indiana Magazine of History* 25 (1929): 1-13.

Schick, Joseph S. "Early Showboat and Circus in the Upper Valley. *Mid-America* 33 (Oct. 1950): 211-225.

Smith, Edward H. "Invention and the Grifter." *Scientific American* 129 (Aug. 1923): 78-79, 135, 142-43.

_____."The Inventor and the Gay Gambler." *Scientific American.* 129 (Sept. 1923): 150-51, 215-16.

Winter, Marian Hannah. "Juba and American Minstrelsy." *Dance Index* 6 (1947): 20-42.

C. Dissertations and Theses

Badal, Robert Samuel. "Kate and Ellen Bateman: A Study in Precocity." Ph.D. diss., Northwestern U, 1971.

Giglio, Mary Elena. "The Terre Haute Grand Opera House, 1897-1898."

Master's Thesis, Indiana State U, 1974.

Kalbfleisch, Marlene. "The Terre Haute Grand Opera House, 1869-1874." Master's Thesis, Indiana State U, 1972.

Weinfeld, Samuel L. "A Survey of Early Theatrical Activity at New Harmony, Indiana." Master's Thesis, Indiana U, 1964.

D. Miscellaneous

Bowerman, Sara G. "John Banvard." *DAB*, Vol. 1.

"John Banvard." *National Cyclopaedia of American Biography*. Vol. V.

Kendrick, William Carnes. "Reminiscences of Old Louisville." Typewritten. Michigan State Library, Department of Education. Lansing, MI [1937].

Letter. Parkinson, Robert L. to Joan Zolbrod. 12 August 1982.

Letter. Tauber, Margery to author. 7 February 1979.

Records of Bureau of Marine Inspection and Navigation, National Archives, Washington, D.C.

Sutherland, Edwin H. "Circus Grift" Typewritten manuscript. [1938?].